WOMEN OF THE NEW TESTAMENT

Their Lives, Our Hope

PÍA SEPTIÉN

Liguori
LIGUORI, MISSOURI

Imprimi Potest:
Harry Grile, CSsR, Provincial
Denver Province, The Redemptorists

Published by Liguori Publications
Liguori, MO 63057-9999

To order, call 800-325-9521, or visit liguori.org.

Library of Congress Cataloging-in-Publication Data

Septién, Pía.
[Mujeres del Nuevo Testamento. English]
Women of the New Testament : their lives, our hope / Pía Septién.—1st ed.
p. cm.
ISBN 978-0-7648-2216-2
1. Women in the Bible—Meditations. 2. Bible. N.T.—Meditations. 3. Catholic Church—Prayers and devotions. I. Title.
BS2445.S3913 2012
225.9'22082—dc23

2012014677

Compliant with *The Roman Missal*, third edition.

Cover design: Pam Hummelsheim Cover image: Steel engraving after a painting by Pietro Benvenuti (Italian painter, 1769–1844), published in 1836.

Liguori Publications, a nonprofit corporation, is an apostolate of The Redemptorists. To learn more about The Redemptorists, visit Redemptorists.com.

Printed in the United States of America.
21 20 19 18 17 / 6 5 4 3 2
First edition

CONTENTS

DEDICATION

The psalm says, children
"are a gift from the LORD" (Psalm 127:3),
and my experience confirms it.
I dedicate this book with all my love
to our four children. I pray every day
that God will grant them the grace
of loving him with all their souls
until the last instant of their lives.
And I thank God for our fifth son, Juan Bosco,
who brought so many lessons of love
to our family during his short life.

INTRODUCTION

This is a continuation of my first book, *Women of the Old Testament*, also published by Liguori Publications. With immense joy, I write this book and hope to help readers encounter the living God.

It is written in the style of an informal heart-to-heart chat. It is not intended to be an academic book, but rather it aims to help us reflect, either individually or as a group, on the lives of some of the women who appear in the New Testament—women who lived in Jesus' time, like Mary Magdalene, or a little while later, like Lydia. Some perhaps knew him personally and spoke with him, like Martha and Mary. Others, like Elizabeth, recognized him as God even before he was born.

As we read along, we will discover what it was that those women saw in Jesus and what led them to follow him. We will also get a glimpse of what he saw in them; for just like us, they were in need of God's love.

This book begins with a chapter dedicated to Mary, the Mother of God and of all humanity, our blessed mother in heaven, so that we will take her example with us as we read the rest of the book.

I.
WOMEN WHO RECOGNIZED GOD IN A LITTLE CHILD

CHAPTER 1

MARY
Mother of Jesus and all people

"We greet you and call upon you with the Angel's words: 'full of grace' (Luke 1:28), the most beautiful name that God himself has called you from eternity. 'Full of grace' are you, Mary, full of divine love [...], providentially predestined to be Mother of the Redeemer and intimately connected to him in the mystery of salvation.

"'Full of grace' are you, Mary, who, welcoming with your 'yes' the Creator's plan, opened to us the path of salvation. Teach us also at your school to say our 'yes' to the Lord's will. Let it be a 'yes' that joins with your own 'yes' without reservations or shadows, a 'yes' that the Heavenly Father willed to have need of in order to beget the new Man, Christ, the one Savior of the world and of history."

POPE BENEDICT XVI TO IMMACULATE MARY
ON THE SPANISH STEPS,
ROME, DECEMBER 8, 2006

Objective

Mary, our blessed mother in heaven, can be studied from very different perspectives since she is the best example of total openness to God's will. In this chapter we will focus on Mary as the Mother of God and as our mother.

Scripture text

- Mary, the Mother of Jesus, in the childhood narratives
  Luke 1:26–56; Luke 2:1–52
- Mary, the Mother of Jesus, at the wedding in Cana.
  John 2:1–12
- Mary, the Mother of Jesus, at the foot of the cross
  John 19:25–30

Introduction to the character

Many books and countless chapters have been written about the Blessed Virgin Mary. God willing, many more are yet to be written!

This book begins with a chapter dedicated to Mary, Mother of Jesus and mother of all people. A beautiful task awaits us! We will read and reflect on Mary's behavior as Jesus' Mother so we can understand how she acts as our mother.

With her example as a loving mother who was always present in the important moments of Jesus' life, she shows us how it is possible to love God above all things and still be present in the lives of the people God has entrusted to us. In Mary's case, that entrusted person was her son, Jesus. In our case, it may be our spouse, children, parents, siblings, friends, colleagues, or acquaintances in the community.

Development of the Bible story

Since the objective of this chapter is to study Mary as the Mother of God and our mother, we will focus on three transcendent moments in her life:

- The annunciation
- The wedding feast in Cana
- Her presence at the foot of the cross

Mary at the annunciation

This exceptionally beautiful Bible story begins with the annunciation of the angel Gabriel to Mary, whose "yes" changed the course of human history. From then on, Mary's life becomes intimately united to Jesus'—and Jesus' life to Mary's.

Three characters in particular comprise this story. A young virgin named Mary; a man named Joseph, of David's lineage and to whom Mary was engaged; and the angel Gabriel, who had been sent by God.

The angel presents himself to Mary and greets her, paying her the most beautiful compliment that a person could ever be given: "Hail, favored one! The Lord is with you" (Luke 1:28). No less than God, Jesus, the Lord of lords and the king of kings, is with you. And besides that, you are the favored one, full of his grace!

Mary was "greatly troubled at what was said and pondered what sort of greeting this might be" (Luke 1:29). Troubled at hearing what the angel said and not at the messenger's presence? This tells us a great deal about Mary's relationship with God. She was probably so close to God that the angel's presence did not worry her, just the message.

The angel answers, "Do not be afraid, Mary" (Luke 1:30). The angel's words continue to be just as fitting today as they were then. "Do not be afraid," God has a plan. Thus, the angel declares, “And behold, Elizabeth, your relative, has also conceived a son in her old age, and this is the sixth month for her who was called barren; for nothing will be impossible for God” (Luke 1:36–37).

Nothing is impossible for God!

Mary at the wedding in Cana

This passage from Jesus’ life is very famous and has been depicted in countless paintings for posterity. Considered the miracle with which Christ began his public life, this passage is frequently read during the rite of Catholic matrimony.

We are told that a wedding was being celebrated in Cana of Galilee and that Mary was there, as well as Jesus and his disciples.

Before continuing with the story, it is necessary to explain that the celebration of a wedding in Jesus’ time was an occasion for great rejoicing, not just for the couple, but for all of the community. A wedding at that time and in that region of the world was a big event, since it not only broke the routine of heavy labor that the people did to survive, but it was also a celebration that strengthened the community. And a very important part of the celebration was the wine that was served at the feast.

Let us continue with the story of this wedding, in which something happened that no one would ever want to happen at his or her own wedding: The wine ran out! That was when Mary, who had realized what was happening, went into action. There are authors who suggest that Mary probably was helping in the kitchen or serving the food when she saw what had happened and immediately turned to her Son, telling him, “They have no wine” (John 2:3b), as if saying, “Do something for this newlywed couple so they can keep celebrating with their guests on this special day.”

Jesus answered, “Woman, how does your concern affect me? My hour has not yet come” (John 2:4). Jesus thinks that the moment has not yet come to reveal himself to all humanity as the one sent by God. But this response does not prevent Mary’s objective from being fulfilled: avoiding letting the newlyweds suffer embarrassment. Firm in her purpose, she tells the servants, “Do whatever he tells you” (John 2:5).

The next verse tells us how Jesus gives instructions to the servants, telling them to fill six jars with water and bring them to the headwaiter, who says in surprise, “Everyone serves good wine first, and then when people have drunk freely, an inferior one; but you have kept the good wine until now” (John 2:10).

On that day, something begins that will henceforth be a constant reality: Mary’s intercession to Jesus for the needs of human beings.

To Jesus through Mary!

Mary at the foot of the cross

The Gospel of John tells us how, at the end of his life, at the moment of the crucifixion, Jesus was accompanied by four women and John the Apostle. All the rest fled!

It tells us, “Standing by the cross of Jesus were his mother and his mother’s sister, Mary the wife of Clopas, and Mary of Magdala” (John 19:25). The Virgin’s presence at the foot of the cross allows us to see her great love for Jesus. There can be no other coherent explanation for the fact that someone would dare to accompany a crucified man in his final moments—no other explanation than love, since only love is capable of being stronger than fear.

Mary stands at her son’s side once more as a companion and witness. With her presence, she supports him and encourages him to fulfill his mission.

But Jesus does not let himself be outdone in generosity, and even in the midst of his great suffering, as he saw his mother and the beloved disciple with her, "he said to his mother, 'Woman, behold, your son.' Then he said to the disciple, 'Behold, your mother.' And from that hour the disciple took her into his home" (John 19:26–27).

What does Mary's story teach us?

- It shows us the greatness of her faith, which led her to say the "yes" that changed human history.
- It teaches us that Mary's response springs from her great faith in God and her intention to be faithful to him always.
- It encourages us to take seriously the angel who declared, "Do not be afraid" (Luke 1:30). This is an important lesson for us as twenty-first-century men and women who are constantly worrying: We worry about what happened, what is happening, and what could happen.
- It reminds us that what happened belongs to the past and we cannot change it, but we can learn from it, and we can do something about what is happening now. As for what will happen in the future, we can do everything possible so that things turn out well.
- It teaches us to get busy and not to fret.
- It helps us value the role Mary played during Jesus' life as she stood by his side.
- It reveals how Mary is in touch with people's needs, and that just as she was attentive to that newlywed couple, she is constantly attentive to us.
- It shows Mary's tenacity as she gently but firmly asks Jesus to act in favor of the newlyweds.
- It shows us that Jesus listens to his mother.
- It helps us see how Mary was present in the joyful and pleasant times of her Son's life, like his birth or the wedding at Cana, and in the hard times like the crucifixion.

- It shows us Mary's fidelity as she stood by her Son to the end.
- It teaches us that love is capable of being stronger than fear. Mary was there, at the foot of the cross.
- It also teaches us how she is our adoptive mother. One of the last things Jesus said before dying was, "Behold your mother" (John 19:26). And the Gospel tells us that from that day on, the disciple took her into his home.
- It teaches us to value Mary as the Mother of God and our mother.

What does the *Catechism of the Catholic Church* tell us?

§148: "The Virgin Mary most perfectly embodies the obedience of faith. By faith Mary welcomes the tidings and promise brought by the angel Gabriel, believing that 'with God nothing will be impossible' (Luke 1:37; see Genesis 18:14)."

§149: "Throughout her life and until her last ordeal (see Luke 2:35), when Jesus her son died on the cross, Mary's faith never wavered. She never ceased to believe in the fulfillment of God's word. And so the Church venerates in Mary the purest realization of faith."

§144: Mary is the perfect model of obedience of faith.

§165: Mary and the saints provide an example of faith.

§437: Jesus Christ was born of Mary.

§456: The Creed says Jesus' incarnation was by the work of the Holy Spirit.

§484: The annunciation to Mary begins "the fullness of time."

§485: Mary conceives the "eternal Son of the Father."

§724: "In Mary, the Holy Spirit manifests the Son of the Father....She is the burning bush of the definitive theophany."

§726: Mary, Mother of the "whole Christ."

§964: She models unity with Jesus.

§2030: She is an example of holiness.
§2617: Mary's prayer as found in Scripture and her radical "yes" to God's plan.
§2619: Mary's canticle, the *Magnificat* and its significance.

Questions and ideas for personal reflection

- Now that I have read about Mary, what have I learned about her way of working? Note well: The question is not about Mary's personal history, which is already familiar to me, but about the love she put into her actions.
- If an angel were to appear to me, what would I do? What would I think? What would surprise me? The appearance of the messenger or the words?
- How much time do I spend worried, fearful, overwhelmed?
- I will take a pen and paper and draw a line down the middle of the page. On one side, I will write down the things that worry me, but which I cannot control, such as whether or not it will rain. And on the other side, I will write down the things I *can* control, such as finishing a job. The point is to realize that I worry about things about which I can do absolutely nothing, so worrying about them gets me nowhere. On the other hand, with the list of things I do have control over, I will see what I can do to take care of them. So instead of worrying, I will work on taking care of things as best I can.
- How is my relationship with Mary? Do I treat her like a mother? Does it make me happy to know that she is looking out for me, just as she did for Jesus?
- What did I learn from each of the three moments of Mary's life that were covered in this chapter? From the annunciation? From the wedding at Cana? From Mary at the foot of the cross?
- What can I do to draw closer to Mary and trust more in her help as my intercessor with Jesus?

Group questions and activities

- What have you learned from Mary?
- What would you think if an angel were to appear to you and say, "Hail, favored one, the Lord is with you" (Luke 1:28)?
- Saint Marcellin Champagnat (1789–1840), a French priest and founder of the Marist Brothers, adopted the motto: "All to Jesus through Mary; all to Mary for Jesus." What does this motto say to you?
- As a group, discuss the following:
    - The past is in the past, and there is nothing we can do to change it. What we *can* do is learn from it, and so we live it with faith.
    - We *can* do something in the present. And so we live it with charity.
    - In the future, we *can* do our part so that things turn out well. And so we live it with hope.
    - How many times have we thought that things are going to happen, and when the time comes, they end up not happening...and we realize we had been wearing ourselves out imagining what they were going to say to us, what we were going to answer, etc.?
- In the Mass, immediately after praying the Our Father, the priest says, "Deliver us, Lord, we pray, from every evil, graciously grant peace in our days, that, by the help of your mercy, we may always be free from sin and safe from all distress, as we await the blessed hope and the coming of our Savior, Jesus Christ." What does this prayer tell us? Do we realize that we are asking Jesus for peace in our life so that we can live free from anxiety, worry, and unrest?
- What do you think about the statement made in this chapter that "love can be stronger than fear"?

- Discuss the following Loreto litanies:
  - Virgin most powerful, pray for us.
  - Virgin most faithful, pray for us.
  - Cause of our joy, pray for us.
  - Gate of heaven, pray for us.
  - Health of the sick, pray for us.
  - Refuge of sinners, pray for us.
  - Comfort of the afflicted, pray for us.
  - Help of Christians, pray for us.

Practical resolutions

- Turn to Mary to ask her to protect us. She went through many problems and difficulties, and she understands us.
- Imitate Mary in her willingness to do what God asks of her.
- Like Mary, be attentive to others' needs.
- Whenever you can, accompany your children in the important moments and decisions of their lives.
- Be at peace knowing that Mary is always present in our lives, just as she was in Jesus' life, both in the happy and enjoyable times like Jesus' birth or the wedding at Cana, and in the hard times such as the crucifixion.
- Pray the rosary with great devotion as a totally Marian prayer.
- Memorize the Litany of Loreto in honor of the Virgin Mary so that you can recite it at any time or place, and so bring the Blessed Virgin to mind.
- Talk to others about Mary, the Mother of God and our mother, and seek out and read Catholic books about Mary.

Prayer of Pope Benedict XVI to Our Lady of Loreto
September 1, 2007

Mary, Mother of the "yes," you listened to Jesus
and know the tone of his voice and the beating of his heart.
Morning Star, speak to us of him,
and tell us about your journey of following him
on the path of faith.
Mary, who dwelt with Jesus in Nazareth,
impress on our lives your sentiments,
your docility, your attentive silence,
and make the Word flourish in genuinely free choices.
Mary, speak to us of Jesus, so that the freshness of our faith
shines in our eyes and warms the hearts of those we meet,
as you did when visiting Elizabeth,
who in her old age rejoiced with you for the gift of life.
Mary, Virgin of the *Magnificat*
help us to bring joy to the world and, as at Cana,
lead every young person involved in service of others
to do only what Jesus will tell them.
Mary, [...] pray that Jesus, dead and Risen,
is reborn in us,
and transforms us in a night
full of light, full of him.
Mary, Our Lady of Loreto, Gate of Heaven,
help us to lift our eyes on high.
We want to see Jesus, to speak with him
to proclaim his love to all.
Amen.

CHAPTER 2

ELIZABETH

Mother of John the Baptist and relative of the Virgin Mary

Lord, you sprinkled the fields with flowers
that fill the air with fragrance and freshness;
you covered the heavens with immense brilliance
and gave the seas their eternal rumbling.
Your unrivaled love shines forth in splendor all around;
the earth proclaims your glory everywhere;
and in the midst of these hymns
that spring up from the world,
I want to raise my joyful voice to you.

OFFERING
AMADO NERVO
MEXICAN POET, 1870–1919

Objective

Elizabeth, the mother of John the Baptist and relative of the Virgin Mary, was the first person who was able to recognize God in a little unborn baby and rejoice in Jesus' presence.

Scripture texts: *Luke 1:5–25*
Luke 1:36
Luke 1:39–45
Luke 1:57–66

Introduction to the character

Luke dedicates the first two chapters of his Gospel to the stories of Jesus' birth and childhood. This is where we hear about Elizabeth, who was the mother of John the Baptist, the wife of Zechariah, and a relative of the Virgin Mary.

The angel Gabriel mentions her to Mary during the annunciation when he says, "And behold, Elizabeth, your relative, has also conceived a son in her old age, and this is the sixth month for her who was called barren; for nothing will be impossible for God" (Luke 1:36–37).

Elizabeth's greatness consists in her being the first person to recognize Jesus as the Lord, even before Christ was born! That was what led her to say to Mary, "Most blessed are you among women, and blessed is the fruit of your womb!" (Luke 1:42). And to wonder, "And how does this happen to me, that the mother of my Lord should come to me?" (Luke 1:43).

Development of the Bible story

Luke begins Elizabeth's story by presenting Zechariah, who was a priest of the division of Abijah and was married to Elizabeth, a daughter of Aaron. Luke tells us the two were righteous and blameless in the eyes of God and faithfully fulfilled his commandments and ordinances. Their sadness came from not having been able to have children, because Elizabeth was sterile and the two were advanced in age.

This is where God enters the action. It happened that Zechariah, a priest in the Temple, was chosen by lot, as was the custom, to go into the sanctuary of the Lord to offer the incense. The people remained in prayer outside. While he was there, the angel of the Lord appeared to him. Upon seeing him, Zechariah was troubled and frightened. The angel told him, "Do not be afraid, Zechariah, because your prayer has been heard. Your wife Elizabeth will bear you a son, and you shall name him John. And you will have joy and gladness, and many will rejoice at his birth, for he will be great in the sight of [the] Lord" (Luke 1:13–15).

The angel also told him of the good that his son would do: "He will turn many of the children of Israel to the Lord their God. He will [...] turn the hearts of fathers toward children and the disobedient to the understanding of the righteous" (Luke 1:16–17) and thus prepare a people fit for the Lord. At that time, Zechariah did not know, as we now know, that his son would be John the Baptist, who would prepare hearts for the coming of Jesus, the Messiah.

Finally, the angel said, "I am Gabriel, who stand[s] before God. I was sent to speak to you and to announce to you this good news" (Luke 1:19). Good news: We love good news!

That is how Elizabeth's pregnancy is announced to us: The elderly, the sterile, the one who could not have children, will now have a child. Once again, we see that nothing is impossible for God!

The angel told Zechariah that because he did not believe in these words, he was going to remain mute until those things took place. Upon leaving the Temple, Zechariah could not talk, and the people understood that he had had a vision.

Not long after, in the city of Nazareth, Mary learned from the angel Gabriel during the annunciation that her relative Elizabeth was expecting a child and that she was in her sixth month of pregnancy. The Gospel of Luke tells us that Mary quickly set out to see her. Upon entering Elizabeth's house and greeting her, the child in Elizabeth's womb leapt for joy, and Elizabeth was filled with the Holy Spirit. That was when Elizabeth spoke the words we know and love so much: "Most blessed are you among women, and blessed is the fruit of your womb!" (Luke 1:42).

We see how Jesus' arrival to Elizabeth's house, even within his mother's womb, was able to transmit the joy of the Messiah's coming. This led Elizabeth to exclaim, full of jubilation, "And how does this happen to me, that the mother of my Lord should come to me? For at the moment the sound of your greeting reached my ears, the infant in my womb leaped for joy. Blessed are you who believed that what was spoken to you by the Lord would be fulfilled!" (Luke 1:43–45).

Elizabeth recognized God in that unborn child!

The story continues. "When the time arrived for Elizabeth to have her child she gave birth to a son. Her neighbors and relatives heard that the Lord had shown his great mercy toward her, and they rejoiced with her" (Luke 1:57–58). When they went to circumcise the child on the eighth day, Elizabeth told those who wanted him to be named Zechariah after his father that the boy's name would be John. At that moment, Zechariah was able to speak again and began blessing God.

We are told, "Then fear came upon all their neighbors, and all these matters were discussed throughout the hill country of Judea. All who heard these things took them to heart, saying, 'What, then, will this child be?' For surely the hand of the Lord was with him" (Luke 1:65–66).

That was how John the Baptist came into the world as the one charged with preparing hearts for the coming of Jesus. "The word of God came to John the son of Zechariah in the desert. He went throughout [the] whole region of the Jordan, proclaiming a baptism of repentance for the forgiveness of sins. [...] I am baptizing you with water, but one mightier than I is coming. I am not worthy to loosen the thongs of his sandals. He will baptize you with the holy Spirit and fire" (Luke 3:2–3, 16).

What does Elizabeth's story teach us?

- It teaches us to recognize God in people, events, and situations when we are least expecting it.
- It teaches us to recognize God in children, in the Lord's little ones, in the vulnerable, and in the most needy.
- It makes us see that Elizabeth, instead of talking about "her" pregnancy, focused on the child Mary bore in her womb. And all the praise was for Jesus, the Word made flesh.
- It teaches us to put the things of God in the first place.
- It encourages us to rejoice at the birth of a new life, just as Elizabeth's neighbors rejoiced.
- It teaches us to rejoice at the mercy God shows in others.
- It teaches us that there is nothing impossible for God. As an example, we have Elizabeth and Zechariah, who had a son in their old age.
- It teaches us to appreciate the Virgin Mary's presence in our lives.

- It shows us how Mary brought her relative Elizabeth to the Messiah through her visit.
- It reminds us of the happiness that comes from trusting in the Lord.
- It also shows us the happiness Mary felt at having trusted in God. True happiness is the fruit of self-giving, since we were made to give, to come out of ourselves, and to give generously to others.
- It shows us how Elizabeth and Zechariah's prayers were heard by God, who in due time fulfilled their hearts' desires.
- It teaches us that God always listens and responds to our supplications, and that sometimes the answer can be "no" or "not now."
- It makes us see how God acts in our lives. Most often we find God in the ordinary, but it can happen that sometimes we will meet the extraordinary, as in the case of the annunciation.
- It shows us that although Luke tells us that Elizabeth and Zechariah were "righteous in the eyes of God, observing all the commandments and ordinances of the Lord blamelessly" (Luke 1:6), they also had their sufferings. No one escapes the mystery of suffering.
- It teaches that God does not ignore our sufferings but brings a greater good out of them.
- It teaches us to be instruments of God.
- It teaches us that, even before Jesus was born, Elizabeth had already recognized him as the "Lord."

What does the *Catechism of the Catholic Church* tell us?

§65 "'In times past, God spoke in partial and various ways to our ancestors through the prophets; in these last days, he spoke to us through a son" (Hebrews 1:1–2). Christ, the Son of God made man, is the Father's one, perfect and unsurpassable Word."

§1 God's Son was sent as the "Redeemer and Savior."

§51 God reveals a loving plan.

§53 Revelation culminates "in the person and mission of the Incarnate Word, Jesus Christ."

§65 Jesus is the Father's "one, perfect, and unsurpassable Word."

§457 Jesus became human to heal our afflictions and reconcile us with the Father, so "we might know God's love" (*CCC* 458), and to be an example or Way of holiness (*CCC* 459).

§464 Jesus is true God and true man.

§476 Jesus was fully human.

§495 Mary is the "'mother of God (*Theotokos*)'."

§522 God prepared us for Jesus' coming through salvation history.

§523 Saint John the Baptist's role.

§1040 At the Final Judgment, we will understand God's providence and the ways of God.

Questions for personal reflection

- "Is anything too marvelous for the LORD to do? At the appointed time, about this time next year, I will return to you, and Sarah will have a son" (Genesis 18:14). What feeling does this verse stir in me? Does it calm me, fill me with peace? Why?

- Elizabeth says, "And how does this happen to me, that the mother of my Lord should come to me?" (Luke 1:43). I can ask myself, how does this happen to me, that the Lord should come to me? What have I done to deserve the privilege of baptism, of the faith?
- When I receive very special news for me and I want to share it, and the other person also has special news that he wants to share, what happens? Does it become a battle to see who gets to talk first? Or do I listen patiently and prudently to what the other person has to tell me?
- Have I had the experience of realizing that the Lord is present in me, in my life, in my family, in my community?
- What did I learn from Elizabeth's words when Mary came to her home?
- Do I have some request in the depths of my heart that I have not presented to God?
- Just as Jesus, while yet inside his mother's womb, prepared John—who was also in Elizabeth's womb—so God prepares us for our mission. What is my mission? Do I know it? Do I intuit it? What has God asked me to do?

Group questions and activities

- What did we learn from Zechariah?
- What did we learn from Elizabeth?
- Why does God sometimes delay in answering our prayers? And why does the Lord sometimes answer with a "no?"
- What have I asked of the Lord that has yet to be fulfilled? What may be God's reason for not responding?
- What is the difference between believing in God and believing God? Could there be many people who believe in God and few who believe God? Why?

- Comment as a group on how God acts in our lives in many ways. Share the ordinary and extraordinary occasions in which God may have acted in your life.
- The prophet Habakkuk writes the following about the petitions we make of God: "How long, O LORD, must I cry for help and you do not listen? Or cry out to you, 'Violence!' and you do not intervene?" (Habakkuk 1:2). God's answer: "For the vision is a witness for the appointed time, a testimony to the end; it will not disappoint. If it delays, wait for it, it will surely come, it will not be late" (Habakkuk 2:3). Do these words give us peace? What is the difference between "God's time" and "humans' time?"

Practical resolutions

- Following Mary's example, I will hasten to help the most needy, those whom society looks down upon.
- It is a fact that I am constantly relating to people. Following Mary's example, when I meet with other people, I will bring them to God by my charity, my understanding words, my good humor and sweetness.
- I will ask Jesus to increase my faith so that I can see his action in my life, both in the little things and in the big things.
- I will ask Jesus to let me see his loving hand in my life, especially in difficult situations.
- Like Mary and Elizabeth, I will celebrate the presence of Jesus in my life.
- I will rejoice at the birth of a baby.
- I will be faithful to what God asks of me, just like Elizabeth and Zechariah, who obeyed God and named the baby John, going against the customs of the time.
- I will know how to wait for *the Lord's time*, which is very different from my time.

Magníficat

A hymn spoken by the Virgin Mary in Elizabeth's presence, praising God for his action in her and in others.

> And Mary said:
> "My soul proclaims the greatness of the Lord;
> my spirit rejoices in God my savior.
> For he has looked upon his handmaid's lowliness;
> behold, from now on will all ages call me blessed.
> The Mighty One has done great things for me,
> and holy is his name.
> His mercy is from age to age
> to those who fear him.
> He has shown might with his arm,
> dispersed the arrogant of mind and heart.
> He has thrown down the rulers from their thrones
> but lifted up the lowly.
> The hungry he has filled with good things;
> the rich he has sent away empty.
> He has helped Israel his servant,
> remembering his mercy,
> according to his promise to our fathers,
> to Abraham and to his descendants forever.

LUKE 1:46–55

CHAPTER 3

ANNA

The prophetess, a woman who was able to recognize God in a newborn baby

There was also a prophetess, Anna, the daughter of Phanuel, of the tribe of Asher. She was advanced in years, having lived seven years with her husband after her marriage, and then as a widow until she was eighty-four. She never left the temple, but worshiped night and day with fasting and prayer. And coming forward at that very time, she gave thanks to God and spoke about the child to all who were awaiting the redemption of Jerusalem.

LUKE 2:36–38

Objective

In a society where youth is considered a divine treasure, where millions of dollars are spent every year to fight aging, erase wrinkles, and cover gray hairs—and where people can do anything and go to the ends of the earth in search of happiness—the prophetess Anna is presented as a reminder of what is truly important: finding God.

Anna, an elderly woman, a widow with a lifestyle that perhaps many would describe as boring, is a sign that "not all that glitters is gold." In the midst of widowhood and service, she found her peace and fulfillment in God. In her old age, she had the opportunity to recognize God and proclaim him to others.

Scripture text: *Luke 2:36–38*

Introduction to the character

Who was the prophetess Anna?

Luke tells us at the beginning of his Gospel that the child Jesus was brought by his parents to the Temple in Jerusalem when the days of purification were fulfilled according to the law of Moses. This law states that every firstborn male shall be consecrated to the Lord (Exodus 13:2) and that the parents were to offer a pair of turtledoves or two pigeons in sacrifice (Leviticus 12:8).

When Joseph, Mary, and Jesus came to the Temple, they met with Anna the prophetess, whom the Gospel of Luke says was an old woman, a descendent of the tribe of Asher. She had been married as a young woman and was widowed after seven years of marriage. Now she was eighty-four years old and was dedicated to serving God day and night with fasting and prayer. She never left the Temple (Luke 2:36–37).

Development of the Bible story

Of the four evangelists, Luke tells us of the encounter between the prophetess Anna and Jesus when he was just a baby. This encounter took place in the Temple of Jerusalem, where Joseph and Mary were taking the child Jesus to present him to the Lord, just as the law required, as found in the Book of Exodus: "Consecrate to me every firstborn; whatever opens the womb among the Israelites, whether of human being or beast, belongs to me" (Exodus 13:2).

They also had to fulfill the precept of the law that said:

> "Tell the Israelites: When a woman has a child, giving birth to a boy, she shall be unclean....On the eighth day, the flesh of the boy's foreskin shall be circumcised, and then she shall spend thirty-three days more in a state of blood purity; she shall not...enter the sanctuary till the days of her purification are fulfilled. When the days of her purification...are fulfilled, she shall bring to the priest at the entrance of the tent of meeting a yearling lamb for a burnt offering and a pigeon or a turtledove for a purification offering. The priest shall offer them before the LORD to make atonement for her, and thus she will be clean again after her flow of blood....If, however, she cannot afford a lamb, she may take two turtledoves or two pigeons."
>
> LEVITICUS 12:2–8

What a beautiful image of a couple that wished to be faithful to God and do what the law required. They went to the Temple of Jerusalem while the boy was still little; the mother had given birth just a few weeks before. The Scripture tells us that they offered "the sacrifice of a pair of turtledoves or two young pigeons, in accordance with the dictate in the law of the Lord" (Luke 2:24).

Here it is worth stopping to put ourselves in Joseph and Mary's place for a moment. How excited they must have been, how enthusiastically they must have gone to the Temple, carrying the baby Jesus in their arms and in their hearts. And what peace that came from knowing they were doing what was required.

Once in the Temple, Luke tells us in his Gospel, they first met the elderly Simeon, to whom it had been "revealed...by the holy Spirit that he should not see death before he had seen the Messiah of the Lord" (Luke 2:26). Thus, upon seeing Jesus, he was filled with joy. In the Temple, they also met Anna, whom Luke tells us was an elderly, widowed prophetess who had been married for seven years in her youth and who had been dedicated for eighty-four years to serving God "night and day with fasting and prayer" (Luke 2:37).

This is the culminating point of our story: Anna's encounter with the baby Jesus!

But...who was Anna? The Gospel tells us that Anna was a prophetess, and that she was elderly, widowed, and a servant of God. What a combination! Let us see, then, what these peculiar characteristics of Anna's are all about. First, let's go deeper with the term "prophetess." To be able to understand this description in its entirety, we have to understand what prophecy meant for the people of Israel: A prophet was a man or woman who spoke of God, who moved consciences, who proclaimed God.

The second description of Anna is that she was elderly. As we all know, old age brings two things: on the one hand, a diminution of physical strength, but on the other, an increase in maturity, wisdom, and good sense. The Book of Sirach explains: "How appropriate is sound judgment in the gray-haired, and good counsel in the elderly! How appropriate is wisdom in the aged, understanding and counsel in the venerable! The crown of the elderly, wide experience; their glory, the fear of the Lord" (Sirach 25:4–6).

In the third place, the text tells us that she was a widow. Being a widow in that time period was very difficult, since it meant being without protection or material resources. If it is difficult today to be unprotected and helpless, it was even more so in those times—and more so for women, who depended totally on the care and protection that men could give them.

Finally, the text tells us that she served God even in the midst of her solitude and suffering both day and night. We can safely say that Anna was a woman dedicated to God and to the things of God.

Luke also tells us that she was a daughter of Phanuel, of the tribe of Asher (Luke 2:36). It was very common in that time period to identify a woman by her relationship to a man: Matthew tells us about the curing of Peter's mother-in-law (Matthew 8:14), of the request that the mother of James and John made to Jesus (Matthew 20:20), of the words spoken to Pilate by his wife (Matthew 27:19). And in the Old Testament, the same happened: We are told of the wife and daughters-in-law of Noah (Genesis 7:6–9), of the daughter of the Pharaoh of Egypt (Exodus 2:1–10), etc. And Anna was not the exception. In the Gospel of Luke, she is immediately identified as the daughter of Phanuel; moreover, the text tells us that she was from the tribe of Asher, one of the twelve tribes of Israel. Anna was part of the people of Israel, a people awaiting the coming of salvation.

Therefore, Anna was a true Israelite who, upon arriving to the Temple and meeting Jesus, began to give "thanks to God and spoke about the child to all who were awaiting the redemption of Jerusalem" (Luke 2:38). She was one of those awaiting the liberation of Jerusalem. She trusted that the Lord would not forget the people of God, and she recognized in that small baby the long-awaited redemption of Israel. Thus, she began giving glory to God and speaking of the child to all who were awaiting the redemption of Israel.

Anna played an important role in salvation history as a messenger of the proclamation of the Messiah's birth. And she confirmed with her words what Simeon had said just a few moments before: This child is the Messiah of the Lord (Luke 2:26). How deeply moved she must have felt when she found the baby Jesus! How deeply moving is the encounter of two souls who have been waiting for each other! That moment must have been something Anna would never forget: her encounter with God!

Sacred Scripture tells us that the visit of Jesus, Mary, and Joseph to the Temple ended when they had fulfilled all that the law of the Lord required. Then they returned to their city of Nazareth.

What does Anna teach us?

- To recognize God in a special way in the most vulnerable. Anna recognized God in a little baby who had been born just a few weeks before.
- That finding God causes great joy, a joy that cannot be compared to human joys, one that brings us peace.
- Anna teaches us never to stop praying, no matter our age, even if we are going through hard times, even though we may be discouraged, even if we think God is not listening to us.
- She shows us how to pray to God both in public and in private. The Lord is to be praised in the Temple and in daily life.
- Anna shows us that there are people who, in spite of the difficulties they have been through in life, do not separate themselves from God.
- She teaches us that it is possible to suffer without growing bitter. Suffering leads some people to separate themselves from God, to harden their hearts, to be resentful and rebel against God. Anna shows us that it is possible to suffer and yet stay close to God.

- The prophetess reminds us that the important thing is how we live through difficult moments in our lives, since sufferings, as we said earlier, either lead us away from God or draw us closer. They can make us nobler, closer to those who suffer, more softhearted, more charitable, and kinder.
- She shows us that in the field of faith, when we face a suffering, we can have two reactions: We can either cling to God and grow deeper in the faith or abandon God and faith.
- Anna also reminds us not to stop hoping. Anna was a woman advanced in age who had spent eighty-four years serving God night and day without leaving the Temple. Yet she had never stopped hoping.
- In summary, Anna the prophetess teaches us to live the virtue of hope.

What does the *Catechism of the Catholic Church* tell us?

§64 Through the prophets God provides hope. "Above all, the poor and humble of the Lord (see Ezekiel 2:3) will bear this hope. Such holy women as Sarah, Rebecca, Rachel, Miriam, Deborah, Hannah, Judith and Esther kept alive the hope of Israel's salvation."

§1818 "The virtue of hope responds to the aspiration to happiness" found in every human heart.

§1843 "By hope we desire, and with steadfast trust await from God, eternal life and the graces to merit it."

§2086 The first commandment is a source of hope.

§2096 Adoring God means recognizing "the Lord and Master of everything that exists, as infinite and merciful Love" and "acknowledging our condition as a creature before the Creator" (*CCC* 2628).

§2657 Prayer is a source of hope.

Questions for personal reflection

- In what events and circumstances of my life have I lost hope?
- Do I know anyone who lives the virtue of hope?
- What do I think of Jesus' words to his disciples: "Do not be afraid?" (Matthew 28:10). Am I afraid right now? Have I lived with fear in the past? Do I fear the future?
- How do I see God? As someone close or distant? As a father or as a judge?
- Am I close to God or distant? What is keeping me from being close to the Lord?
- Mary and Joseph fulfilled their commitment to go to the Temple for the presentation of Jesus and for Mary's purification. Do I fulfill my commitments: my commitments as a Christian and my commitments as a citizen of the world, as a member of a family?
- Anna recognized the Messiah in a small baby, seeing in Jesus the salvation promised by God to all people. Am I capable of seeing God in the most needy people? In those whom society considers less important?

Group questions and activities

- What have we learned from the prophetess Anna?
- Joseph and Mary brought Jesus to the Temple to fulfill the law of Moses. With this attitude, they show us their readiness to follow God's laws and precepts. What do we think about their actions?
- The First Letter of John says, "We have come to know and to believe in the love God has for us. God is love, and whoever remains in love remains in God and God in him" (1 John 4:16). How can we remain in love?
- "There is no fear in love, but perfect love drives out fear" (1 John 4:18). Explain what John means by this sentence. Why does he say that there is no fear in love, and that perfect love drives out fear?

- In his Letter to the Romans, Saint Paul tells us, "For you did not receive a spirit of slavery to fall back into fear, but you received a spirit of adoption, through which we cry, 'Abba, Father!'" (Romans 8:15). How can we avoid falling back into fear? What can we do to trustingly call God "Father?"

Practical resolutions

- What am I going to do now that I have read about Anna's way of acting? What did I learn from her actions?
- I will strive to live with hope, putting my trust in God, my Creator. I will cast discouragement aside.
- I will try to talk to others about what the virtue of trust means.
- Like Joseph and Mary, I will fulfill the precepts of the law of God, so I will study the Ten Commandments and their scope. It would be good to investigate what the *Catechism of the Catholic Church* says about what each of the Ten Commandments entails. The following numbers cover them: 2083 to 2557. It is worth reading them because of the richness of their content.
- I will also fulfill the five commandments of the Catholic Church. Although they are listed here, it would be worthwhile to read about them in these numbers of the *Catechism of the Catholic Church*: 2042 to 2043.
- Attend the entire Mass on Sundays and other holy days of obligation, and refrain from heavy labor.
- Go to confession at least once a year.
- Receive the sacrament of the Eucharist at least on Easter.
- Abstain from eating meat and fast on the days established by the Church.
- Help the Church in its needs.

Prayer

Psalm 71

In you, LORD, I take refuge; let me never be put
to shame. […]
Be my rock of refuge, my stronghold to give me safety;
for you are my rock and fortress. […]
You are my hope, Lord; my trust, GOD, from my youth.
On you I have depended since birth;
from my mother's womb you are my strength;
my hope in you never wavers.
My mouth shall be filled with your praise,
shall sing your glory every day.
Do not cast me aside in my old age; as my strength fails,
do not forsake me. […]
God, be not far from me; my God, hasten to help me.
[…]
I will always hope in you and add to all your praise.
My mouth shall proclaim your just deeds,
day after day your acts of deliverance,
though I cannot number them all.
I will speak of the mighty works of the Lord; O GOD,
I will tell of your singular justice.
God, you have taught me from my youth;
to this day I proclaim your wondrous deeds.
Now that I am old and gray, do not forsake me, God,
that I may proclaim your might
to all generations yet to come, your power and justice,
God,
to the highest heaven.

You have done great things; O God, who is your equal?
Turn and comfort me, that I may praise you with the lyre
for your faithfulness, my God, and sing to you
with the harp, O Holy One of Israel!
My lips will shout for joy as I sing your praise;
my soul, too, which you have redeemed.
Yes, my tongue shall recount your justice day by day.

II.
WOMEN WHO RECOGNIZED THE GREATNESS OF GOD

CHAPTER 4

THE WIDOW'S OFFERING

The woman who placed two coins —all she had to live on— in the Temple treasury

He sat down opposite the treasury and observed how the crowd put money into the treasury. Many rich people put in large sums. A poor widow also came and put in two small coins worth a few cents. Calling his disciples to himself, he said to them, "Amen, I say to you, this poor widow put in more than all the other contributors to the treasury. For they have all contributed from their surplus wealth, but she, from her poverty, has contributed all she had, her whole livelihood."

MARK 12:41–44

"Therefore I tell you, do not worry about your life, what you will eat [or drink], or about your body, what you will wear. Is not life more than food and the body more than clothing? Look at the birds in the sky; they do not sow or reap, they gather nothing into barns, yet your heavenly Father feeds them. Are not you more important than they?"

MATTHEW 6:25–26

Objective

In our lives, the concern for having a good reputation, the desire to have the affection of relatives and friends, material goods, and respect, and the need to come off well before others are always there. When any of these is missing, we lose sleep and sometimes our appetite, until our hair falls out due to anxiety. We get stomach pains, get upset easily, and end up always dreaming of receiving hugs and applause from others, and even of winning the lottery. And if we add to this the fact that we live in a society where accumulating material goods, being the best, having more, being the most-loved, and being the most well-known are not only highly valued but actively encouraged. Recall that this old widow, who gave everything she had to God, sets an example for us of totality: total trust in God's providence and total self-giving.

Scripture text: *Mark 12:41–44*
Luke 21:1–4

Introduction to the character

Who was the widow who placed everything she had to live on in the Temple treasury?

Both the Gospels of Mark and Luke tell us how Jesus warned his listeners to watch out for the teachers of the law who sought all kinds of honors for themselves. And by contrast he presented them with the example of a widow who was standing in front of them, placing her contribution in the Temple treasury. Jesus told them, "I tell you truly, this poor widow put in more than all the rest; for those others have all made offerings from their surplus wealth, but she, from her poverty, has offered her whole livelihood" (Luke 21:3–4). She gave everything because her heart was overflowing with love.

Development of the Bible story

Jesus' encounter with the widow took place while he was teaching in the Temple, where many people went to listen to him "with delight" (Mark 12:37). On this occasion, Jesus told his disciples in front of the people who were listening, "Be on guard against the scribes, who like to go around in long robes and love greetings in marketplaces, seats of honor in synagogues, and places of honor at banquets. They devour the houses of widows and, as a pretext, recite lengthy prayers. They will receive a very severe condemnation" (Luke 20:46–47).

As a good teacher, Jesus did not let the opportunity to form his listeners' hearts pass by. And thus, as a contrast to the haughty airs of the teachers of the law, Jesus presents the simplicity and integrity of a woman who was just then depositing her offering in the Temple treasury.

This woman was surely not the only person to deposit money in the Temple treasury while Jesus was there, but she was the one who caught Jesus' eye. The others' offerings did not surprise him, since Jesus knew that they gave from their surplus; he knew that they had not sacrificed to make their contribution to the Temple. But in spite of her extreme poverty, this widow gave what little she had, and that little bit was all she had to live on.

It is worth pausing here to explain that for the Hebrew people, the widows, orphans, and foreigners were considered the most vulnerable people in their society, since they had no other human being to look out for them. Deuteronomy tells us that God "executes justice for the orphan and the widow, and loves the resident alien, giving them food and clothing" (Deuteronomy 10:18) and in the Second Book of Samuel, we are told how the widow of Tekoa "went to the king and fell to the ground in homage, saying, 'Help, O king!' The king said to her, 'What do you want?' She replied: 'Alas, I am a widow; my husband is dead. Your servant had two sons, who quarreled in the field, with no one to part them, and one of them struck his brother and killed him'" (2 Samuel 14:4–6).

Let's return to our story. This woman, who deposited all she had to live on in the Temple treasury, shows us that God's ways of reckoning are different from the world's. The world's way tells us that the bigger the number, the larger the amount. With his reckoning, Jesus tells us that even if the number is smaller, the person's generosity, detachment, and trust in God is what makes the amount large. The widow's offering comes from a heart full of love for God, in whom she abandons herself. It is her faith that sustains her and gives her courage to trust in God, who is always faithful and who will take care of her needs.

When someone has a personal relationship with God, the entrusted self-giving is spontaneous and can become sacrificial. That's what we see in the case of this generous woman. Her offering comes from a heart that loves and loves greatly, to the point that she gives from her poverty all she has to live on. But that love is also full of trust: She trusts in the love of God, in Yahweh's divine providence, and she knows that he, the king of kings and Lord of lords, will take care of her.

Jesus tells us: "So do not worry and say, 'What are we to eat?' or 'What are we to drink?' or 'What are we to wear?' All these things the pagans seek. Your heavenly Father knows that you need them all. But seek first the kingdom (of God) and his righteousness, and all these things will be given you besides. Do not worry about tomorrow; tomorrow will take care of itself. Sufficient for a day is its own evil" (Matthew 6:31–33).

What do we learn from the woman who put all she had to live on in the Temple treasury?

- She teaches us there are people who are convinced that God takes care of his own.
- Not to stop doing good simply because we cannot do much. Although it is a small contribution, Jesus appreciates it.
- The poor widow shows us the importance of "the spirit with which we give." Not just money, but affection, time, teaching, etc.
- She helps us see what a heart overflowing with love is capable of doing.
- She encourages us not to stop doing good just because it is difficult or involves sacrifice.
- She teaches us to give, and to give not just from our surplus, but to give what we need to live on.
- This poor widow gives us a clear example of how people act when they trust totally in God.
- With her attitude, she reminds us of Jesus' words when he told us not to be worried about what we will eat or drink, not to afflict ourselves, and to seek first God's reign and his justice, and the rest will be given to us (Luke 12:29–31).
- She lets us see how far abandonment in God's hands can go, an abandonment that led her to throw into the Temple treasury all she had to live on.
- She teaches us what totality is. Everything for God.
- She shows us a detached heart.
- She teaches us what a soul does when it truly knows God.
- She shows us what it means to believe in God and *believe* God.
- In short, she teaches us to trust in the Lord.

What does the *Catechism of the Catholic Church* tell us?

§321 All creatures are guided by God's providence "with wisdom and love to their ultimate end."

§322 "Christ invites us to filial trust in the providence of our heavenly Father (see Matthew 6:26–34)."

§308 God acts through the people of God and all humanity.

§307 Humans share in God's providence.

§302 God protects and governs all "toward an ultimate perfection to be attained."

§2830 God sustains us.

Questions for personal reflection

- Am I always worried about tomorrow and about what is going to happen? Or do I live trusting in the words of Christ who tells us, "Do not worry about tomorrow; tomorrow will take care of itself. Sufficient for a day is its own evil" (Matthew 6:34)?
- Jesus said, "As for you, do not seek what you are to eat and what you are to drink, and do not worry anymore. All the nations of the world seek for these things, and your Father knows that you need them. Instead, seek his kingdom, and these other things will be given you besides" (Luke 12:29–31).
  What afflicts me?
- What worries me so much that it makes me unable to put the reign of God in the first place?
- The Letter to the Hebrews tells us, "Let your life be free from love of money but be content with what you have, for he has said, 'I will never forsake you or abandon you.' Thus we may say with confidence: 'The Lord is my helper, I will not be afraid. What can anyone do to me'" (Hebrews 13:5–6)?
- Do I believe that God will never abandon me?
- Do I say with confidence: "The Lord is my helper, I will not be afraid" (Hebrews 13:6)?

- Do I believe that humans can do more than God (Hebrews 13:6)?
- In what circumstances and events of my life have I felt taken care of by God?
- When I give, with what spirit do I act? Am I generous so that people see and admire me? Giving is not just about money, but also about affection, time, kindness, etc.
- Do I truly detach myself like the widow in the Temple, or do I just give from my extra time, talents, and treasures?
- Do I know someone who is just as detached as the widow?

Group questions and activities

- What have we learned from the woman who put all she had to live on in the Temple treasury?
    - In his treatise on the Creed, Saint Thomas Aquinas used an example of medicine to explain God's treatment of the people. In medicine, if a person goes to visit a doctor, he or she will not always understand the ways of the physician (especially in Aquinas' time). However, a physician knows the best treatment. It is the same with God. We must trust that our Divine Physician knows what is best for our personal needs.
    - The same happens to us: we often do not understand that God is acting with infinite providence.
    - What do you think about the following statement: We human beings do not understand how God acts?
    - Share with the group some situation that you have gone through in your life in which at first you did not understand why things were happening that way, but in time, you realized that it was the best thing that could have happened to you, and that God was behind all those events.

- ▸ As a group, discuss the following quote from the Gospel of Matthew:

  "Why are you anxious about clothes? Learn from the way the wild flowers grow. They do not work or spin. But I tell you that not even Solomon in all his splendor was clothed like one of them. If God so clothes the grass of the field, which grows today and is thrown into the oven tomorrow, will he not much more provide for you, O you of little faith?"

  MATTHEW 6:28–30

- ▸ Read the following passage from the Gospel of Luke:

  "As for you, do not seek what you are to eat and what you are to drink, and do not worry anymore. All the nations of the world seek for these things, and your Father knows that you need them. Instead, seek his kingdom, and these other things will be given you besides."

  LUKE 12:29–31

  - ▹ What does it mean to seek the kingdom of God in our lives?

- ▸ The prophet Isaiah tells us:

  Ah! Those who enact unjust statutes,
who write oppressive decrees,
Depriving the needy of judgment,
robbing my people's poor of justice,
Making widows their plunder,
and orphans their prey!
What will you do on the day of punishment,
when the storm comes from afar?
To whom will you flee for help?

  ISAIAH 10:1–4

  - ▹ What do you think of his words?
  - ▹ What do they make you feel?

Practical resolutions

- What does all of the above call me to do?
- Trust in God's providence and care for all creatures.
- Abandon myself into God's hands, just like the woman who put all she had to live on in the Temple treasury.
- Give thanks to God for having given us his Son, who came to teach us what is truly important in God's eyes and who told us in the Sermon on the Mount: "But seek first the kingdom (of God) and his righteousness, and all these things will be given you besides" (Matthew 6:33).
- Don't worry, keep busy.
- Trust in Jesus' words, since believing in Jesus means, "Whatever you ask in my name, I will do" (John 14:13).
- "And I will ask the Father, and he will give you another Advocate to be with you always" (John 14:16).
- "Peace I leave with you; my peace I give to you....Do not let your hearts be troubled or afraid" (John 14:27).
- Give my time, talents, and treasure toward building the kingdom of heaven.
- When I start to worry, remember the widow who trusted totally in God.
- Understand that no one gives more than the one who keeps nothing for himself.

Psalm 23

The LORD is my shepherd;
there is nothing I lack.
In green pastures he makes me lie down;
to still waters he leads me;
he restores my soul.

He guides me along right paths
for the sake of his name.
Even though I walk through the valley
of the shadow of death,
I will fear no evil, for you are with me;
your rod and your staff comfort me.

You set a table before me
in front of my enemies;
You anoint my head with oil;
my cup overflows.

Indeed, goodness and mercy will pursue me
all the days of my life;
I will dwell in the house of the LORD
for endless days.

CHAPTER 5

MARTHA AND MARY

Friends of Jesus

"What have I that you seek my friendship?
What interest do you pursue, my Jesus,
That at my door, covered with dew,
You spend the dark winter nights?

O, how hard was my heart,
For I did not open to you! What strange delirium
If by my ingratitude, the cold ice
Dried the wounds of your pure feet!

How many times the angel told me:
"Look out the window now;
You will see with how much love he persists"!

And how many times, sovereign beauty,
Did I answer, "Tomorrow I will open to you,"
Only to say the same tomorrow!"

Lope de Vega, Spanish poet (1562–1635)

Objective

We spend days and years searching for happiness, looking for the way to live a complete life. Jesus also wants us to live a fulfilled life. He tells us, " I came so that they might have life and have it more abundantly" (John 10:10). And for that to happen, for us to have an abundant life, Jesus gives us the recipe: He tells us that only one thing is necessary. What is it? Let's continue with the story.

Scripture text: *Luke 10:38–42*

Introduction to the characters

The Gospel passage we will be analyzing is short, but very rich in teachings.

Martha and Mary were sisters who received Jesus into their home. While he was there, a typical situation happened: One member of the family was doing all the work of preparing the food and organizing the get-together, while the other member of the family did nothing. As one might expect, there was some friction.

Martha, annoyed with her sister, Mary, for not helping out, turned to Jesus hoping that he would correct Mary. What a surprise Jesus' response must have been for her! "Martha, Martha, you are anxious and worried about many things. There is need of only one thing. Mary has chosen the better part and it will not be taken from her" (Luke 10:41–42).

Development of the Bible story

This brief passage, which is only five verses long, includes so many teachings. It teaches us about friendship with Jesus, service, the work of the home, and above all, it speaks to us about what Jesus considers truly important.

Let us start, then, with this short story. In the time and region of the world where Jesus lived, hospitality—that is, receiving a guest into one's own home and treating him well—was a great virtue. It was a virtue that Martha put into practice when she received Jesus into her home.

Surely, Martha would have gotten to work organizing and preparing everything that was needed to receive Jesus in a suitable way according to the Jewish norms of hospitality, while her sister Mary remained seated at Jesus' feet, listening to him speak. At that time, sitting at the teacher's feet meant sitting to learn from him, and it was common. In the Acts of the Apostles, we are told that Saint Paul sat at the feet of the teacher Gamaliel to be instructed in the law (Acts 22:3).

While Mary learned from Jesus, Martha was busy with many chores. Coming up to Jesus, she told him, "Lord, do you not care that my sister has left me by myself to do the serving? Tell her to help me" (Luke 10:40). This scene could stir up different emotions in us as readers. Some of us might think, *Mary was right to be angry with her sister, since she wasn't helping her.* Others might speculate, *Poor Jesus, he was probably tired after his trip and then he had to referee a squabble between sisters.*

For us, the important thing is to know what Jesus thought when he answered, "Martha, Martha, you are anxious and worried about many things. There is need of only one thing. Mary has chosen the better part and it will not be taken from her" (Luke 10:41–42).

Jesus told Martha that because she was rushing around busy and worried about a thousand things she was losing herself in them. By contrast, Mary had chosen the better part. We note that he did not say Martha was wrong and Mary was right; he just said that Mary had chosen the better part, which consists of being close to him.

What does the story of Jesus' visit to the home of these sisters tell us?

- Only one thing is necessary to live a full, fruitful, and meaningful life: keeping close to Jesus at all times.
- Our work at home, on the job, or at school, etc., should not prevent us from being in touch with Jesus and with our brothers and sisters, starting with the members of our own family, since charity begins at home.
- Jesus appreciates that we are by his side.
- It illustrates the clash of two different temperaments: Martha was hard-working, active, and energetic; Mary was naturally more calm, serene, and peaceful. Jesus does not say that one temperament is better than another; God created both of them. What is better is to choose to be close to Jesus.
- It reminds us of the greatness of human freedom. Mary freely chose to stay at Jesus' feet.
- It teaches us that whenever we choose Jesus, we choose to extend his reign among humanity.
- It teaches us that we can or should do many good things, but not to lose sight of our goal: loving God above all things.
- It reminds us of the greatness of the Eucharist—the best way of being with Jesus!
- It teaches us that if we get distracted with serving, we may end up forgetting whom we are serving.
- It reminds us that Jesus likes us to work for him, but he likes it even better when we love him.
- It reminds us that Jesus is less interested in our report of achievements, successes, and gains than in the love we put into our actions.
- It reminds us that Jesus became man to be with us, to be available to us, to offer us his friendship.

What does the *Catechism of the Catholic Church* tell us?

Friendship with God

§142 “The invisible God, from the fullness” of love greets us as friends in Divine Revelation.

§277 “By grace,” God delivers us from our sins and restores our friendship with the Blessed Trinity.

§355 Humanity is made in God’s image and likeness.

§374 We were created as friends of God.

§396 Freedom is necessary in relationship to the Creator.

§1395 Friendship with Christ is known in the Eucharist.

§1468 The effect of the sacrament of reconciliation is to restore friendship with God.

§1972 Christ’s “law of love” and intimate union with God.

§2567 God invites, we respond.

Prayer

§2560 Jesus reveals himself in prayer.

§2562 “It is the heart that prays. If our heart is far from God, the words of prayer are in vain.”

§2563 “Only the Spirit of God can fathom the human heart and know it fully.”

§2564 Prayer is a “covenant relationship.”

§2566 Humanity seeks God.

§2709 Definition of prayer as given by Saint Teresa of Ávila.

Questions for personal reflection

- Jesus says, "Martha, Martha, you are anxious and worried about many things. There is need of only one thing. Mary has chosen the better part and it will not be taken from her" (Luke 10:41–42). What about me? What am I anxious and worried about? What prevents me from choosing the better part?
- Am I more like Martha or Mary?
- Write a prayer of thanksgiving to Jesus for having stayed with us in the Eucharist.
- The Our Father says, "thy kingdom come, thy will be done." What is God's will in my life?
- Do I really want God's will to be done in my life?
- Jesus said, "I am the vine, you are the branches. Whoever remains in me and I in him will bear much fruit, because without me you can do nothing" (John 15:5).
- What can I do to stay close to Jesus?
- What am I going to do to choose the better part?

Group questions and activities

- What have we learned from Mary?
- What have we learned from Martha?
- What have we learned from Jesus?
- Jesus tells Martha, "You are anxious and worried about many things: There is need of only one thing." What are those things that keep us from listening to Jesus?
- Have you ever had someone stay as a guest for a long time at your house? Under what circumstances?
- Have you ever stayed as a guest for a long time at someone else's house? Under what circumstances?

- In his First Letter to the Corinthians, Saint Paul says, "I am telling you this for your own benefit....for the sake of propriety and adherence to the Lord without distraction" (1 Corinthians 7:35).
- What does he mean by "for the sake of propriety?"
- What does he mean when he says "for the sake of...adherence to the Lord without distraction?"
- Number 24 of the encyclical *Laborem Exercens* (on human work) by Pope John Paul II talks about the spirituality of work. It tells us that work helps "all people to come closer, through work, to God, the Creator and Redeemer, to participate in his salvific plan for man and the world and to deepen their friendship with Christ in their lives."
- Why does he say that work helps people draw closer to God?
- How do people participate in God's salvific plan through work?
- Why does he say that work helps people deepen their friendship with God?

Practical resolutions

- Ask Jesus to help me choose *the better part*, the one that no one can take away from me.
- Arrive early to Mass, sit in a place that helps me pay attention, attentively follow the readings, and participate actively in the responses and songs—in short, do everything I can to be close to Jesus.
- Prepare myself before receiving the Eucharist. Be aware of the person I am going to receive. In the last section of this chapter, titled "Prayer," there is a prayer that can be said to help prepare myself to receive Jesus in the Eucharist.
- Read the Gospels at length and with faith, seeking to know Jesus better and better.

- Ask someone I trust to recommend some books I can read that will help me know and love Jesus more.
- Understand that some people are more active by nature, while others are calmer. God made us that way.
- If I am a person who tends to be active, I will try to understand that there are people who prefer tranquility; on the other hand, if I am a person who prefers silence and reflection, I will not look down on active people.
- Focus on Jesus and his reign, rather than on myself and my achievements.

Prayer

Below are several prayers that we can pray during the day, depending on what activity we are doing, with the goal of keeping God present in our actions.

Daily offering

Lord Jesus:
Dear Lord, I give you my hands to do your work;
I give you my feet to go your way;
I give you my eyes to see as you see;
I give you my tongue to speak your words;
I give you my mind that you may think in me;
I give you my spirit that you may pray in me.
Above all, I give you my heart that you may love in me—
love the Father and love all humankind.
I give you my whole self, Lord, that you may grow in me,
so that it is you who lives, works, and prays in me.
Amen.

Act of Consecration to the Blessed Virgin Mary

O my lady, O my mother!
I dedicate myself entirely to you,
And as proof of my filial affection,
I consecrate to you on this day
My eyes, ears, tongue, and heart:
In a word, my entire being.
And since I am all yours,
O mother of goodness,
Keep and protect me as your own child.
Amen.

Prayer before receiving Communion

I wish, Lord, to receive you with the purity, humility and devotion, with which your most holy Mother received you, with the spirit and fervor of the saints. Lord Jesus Christ, Son of the living God, who, by the will of the Father and the work of the Holy Spirit, through your death gave life to the world, free me by this, your most holy Body and Blood, from all my sins and from every evil; keep me always faithful to your commandments, and never let me be parted from you. Amen.

Prayer before studying

Lord, you make eloquent the tongues of infants.
Refine my speech and pour forth upon my lips
the goodness of your blessing.
Grant to me keenness of mind,
capacity to remember,
skill in learning,
subtlety to interpret,
and eloquence in speech.
May you guide the beginning of my work,
direct its progress,
and bring it to completion.
You who are true God and true man,
Who live and reign, world without end.
Amen.

Saint Thomas Aquinas (1225–1274),
Italian priest and member of the
Order of Preachers (Dominicans)

Prayers before and after eating

Before eating

Bless us, O Lord, and these thy gifts
which from your goodness we are about to receive.
Through Christ our Lord.
Amen.

Another prayer that can be used to bless the meal

I give you thanks, great Lord, for life and sustenance.
You give to us because of who you are, not because I deserve it.
Amen.

After eating

We give you thanks, Lord, for all your gifts, you who live and reign for ever and ever.
Amen.

Night prayer

I adore you, my God,
and I love you with all my heart.
I thank You for having created me,
made me a Christian,
and kept me this day.
Pardon me the evil I have done,
and if I have done some good, accept it.
Take care of me while I sleep
and deliver me from all danger.
May your grace be always with me
and with all my loved ones.
Amen.

Spontaneous prayers

Spontaneous prayers are small prayers that we say during the day to God the Creator, Jesus Christ, the Blessed Virgin, or the saints to keep ourselves in their presence throughout the day. Some people describe them as love arrows shot at God or as compliments for the Blessed Virgin. Their purpose is to keep our mind and heart from drifting away from God.

Some spontaneous prayers follow:

Sacred Heart of Jesus,
I trust in you.

Sacred Heart of Jesus,
forgive us and be our King.

Jesus meek and humble of heart,
make my heart more like Yours.

Sacred Heart of Jesus,
protect our families.

May the loving heart of Jesus in the Blessed Sacrament
be ever praised in heaven and on earth.

Long live Christ the King!

We adore you, O Christ, and we bless you,
who by your Holy Cross redeemed the world.

Praised be Jesus Christ
for ever and ever.

Lord, grant them eternal rest
and may your perpetual light shine upon them.

The Lord is my shepherd,
I lack for nothing.

Lord, increase my faith.

Lord, You know everything. You know that I love You.

I believe, Lord, but help my unbelief.

Jesus, my God, I love You above all things.

My Jesus, have mercy on me.

I am Yours, and for You I was born:
Jesus, what do you want of me?

Holy Spirit, source of light,
enlighten us!

Holy Spirit, sweet guest of my soul,
remain in me and may I remain always in You.

Jesus, Mary, and Joseph,
I give you my heart and soul.

Jesus, Mary, and Joseph,
help me in my final agony.

Jesus, Mary, and Joseph,
may my soul rest in peace with you.

Hail, Mary Most Holy,
Conceived without sin.

Mary, Mother of Grace, Mother of Mercy,
In life and in death, protect us, great Lady.

Holy Mary of Guadalupe,
Pray for us.

Holy Mary of Guadalupe,
Save our country and keep our faith.

Mother of the Divine Word,
Lead us along the right path and be our salvation.

Pray for us, Holy Mother of God,
That we may be made worthy of the promises of Our Lord Jesus Christ.

Sweet Heart of Mary,
Be my salvation.

Most Holy Trinity, one God;
I believe in You, I hope in You, I love You above all else.

CHAPTER 6

LYDIA

A woman who opened her heart and her home to Jesus

"During the night Paul had a vision. A Macedonian stood before him and implored him with these words, 'Come over to Macedonia and help us.' When he had seen the vision, we sought passage to Macedonia at once, concluding that God had called us to proclaim the good news to them. We set sail from Troas, making a straight run for Samothrace, and on the next day to Neapolis, and from there to Philippi, a leading city in that district of Macedonia and a Roman colony. We spent some time in that city. On the sabbath we went outside the city gate along the river where we thought there would be a place of prayer. We sat and spoke with the women who had gathered there. One of them, a woman named Lydia, a dealer in purple cloth, from the city of Thyatira, a worshiper of God, listened, and the Lord opened her heart to pay attention to what Paul was saying. After she and her household had been baptized, she offered us an invitation, 'If you consider me a believer in the

Lord, come and stay at my home,' and she prevailed on us. [...] After inflicting many blows on them, they threw them into prison and instructed the jailer to guard them securely. [...] When they had come out of the prison, they went to Lydia's house where they saw and encouraged the brothers, and then they left."

ACTS 16:9–15, 23, 40

Objective

In our times, where we live at a fast pace because of our jobs, family, commitments, and so on, many people try not to show their skills in the community so that they will not get asked to do something or get put in charge of some project. At that time, Lydia was an example of a follower of Jesus who put the talents God gave her at the service of others, thus helping the early Christian community.

Scripture text: *Acts 16:12–15, 40*

Introduction to the character

Who was Lydia?

Lydia was a woman who dedicated herself to selling purple cloth. While in the city of Philippi, she had the opportunity to listen to Paul and his companions as they spoke about Jesus. Sacred Scripture tells us that the Lord touched her heart so that she could accept Paul's words, and the result was a conversion that led her to get baptized, along with her whole family, and to invite Paul and his companions to stay at her house (Acts 16:14–15).

What generosity and openness Lydia showed! Jesus came into her life and she changed! She listened to Paul, got baptized along with her family, and invited some men from abroad who were traveling throughout the world preaching the message of Jesus to stay at her home. Her generous hospitality came from her conversion. And her conversion—what joy it must have given her! It was the joy that comes from knowing God.

But, who was Lydia and how did she come to listen to Saint Paul speaking about Jesus?

As in any good story, there were various events surrounding this conversion, and it was precisely these small but big happenings that made it possible for the larger story to unfold. Some call them coincidences, but we call them "God-incidences."

Everything begins with Saint Paul who, after having been a major persecutor of the first followers of Jesus, became one of Christ's main apostles. The Acts of the Apostles tells us that Paul, "still breathing murderous threats against the disciples of the Lord, went to the high priest and asked him for letters to the synagogues in Damascus, that, if he should find any men or women who belonged to the way, he might bring them back to Jerusalem in chains. On his journey, as he was nearing Damascus, a light from the sky suddenly flashed around him. He fell to the ground and heard a voice saying to him, 'Saul, Saul, why are you persecuting me?' He said, 'Who are you, sir?' The reply came, 'I am Jesus, whom you are persecuting. Now get up and go into the city and you will be told what you must do.' The men who were traveling with him stood speechless, for they heard the voice but could see no one. Saul got up from the ground, but when he opened his eyes he could see nothing; so they led him by the hand and brought him to Damascus. For three days he was unable to see, and he neither ate nor drank."

Once converted, there was no stopping Paul! He dedicated

himself to traveling so as to bring the message of Jesus to as many people as possible. He himself tells us in his Letter to the Philippians that "whatever gains I had, these I have come to consider a loss because of Christ" (Philippians 3:7). Christ was his gain. Christ conquered his life, his thoughts, and above all, his heart. He could do no less than to share Jesus with others, no less than to evangelize! Saint Jerome tells us, "The world will never see another man of Paul's stature."

And so Paul and his traveling companions, also great men who were convinced of Jesus and his message, set out on their path, obeying Jesus' request to invite the nations to convert (see Luke 24:47b).

On this occasion, they went to Troas, and during the night Paul had a vision in which he saw an inhabitant of Macedonia asking him to come to his city and help them. The Book of the Acts of the Apostles tells us that when he awoke, Paul told his companions about the vision, and they understood that the Lord was the one guiding them to Macedonia so that it could be evangelized (Acts 16:9).

They set out for the island of Samothrace, then went on to Neapolis, until they reached Philippi, one of the main cities of the region of Macedonia and a Roman colony (Acts 16:12). As a Roman colony, Philippi was a leading city in the region. It is worth noting that this geographical region is on the European continent; that is, Paul left Asia Minor, which had been his main mission ground, to break into new lands—Europe itself—in obedience to Jesus' missionary mandate: "Go, therefore, and make disciples of all nations, baptizing them in the name of the Father, and of the Son, and of the holy Spirit" (Matthew 28:19).

The Book of the Acts of the Apostles continues by telling us that once they reached Philippi, they stayed there for a few days, and on Saturday they went outside the city gate "along the river where we thought there would be a place of prayer. We sat and spoke with the women who had gathered there. One of them, a woman named Lydia, a dealer in purple cloth, from the city of Thyatira, a worshiper of God, listened" (Acts 16:13–14). It seems that in Philippi there was no synagogue where the Jews could get together on Saturday, the day of the Lord, to pray. For this reason, they gathered at the banks of the river, which provided the necessary water for the washing, which was an essential part of the Saturday ritual. What a beautiful image: the community gathered along the banks of the river to worship the Lord!

Among the members of that community was Lydia, whose heart "the Lord opened [...] to pay attention to what Paul was saying" (Acts 16:14). She was baptized along with her family and then asked them, "If you consider me a believer in the Lord, come and stay at my home" (Acts 16:15). We can definitely say that Lydia was a woman of action. As the saying goes, "she put her money where her mouth was." She converted and immediately acted, opening the doors of her house so that the men who had led her to believe in Christ could stay at her home.

The Acts of the Apostles continues by telling us about Paul's comings and goings in Philippi. It turned out that a young woman was following them through the streets, shouting, "These people are slaves of the Most High God, who proclaim to you a way of salvation." She did this for many days. Paul became annoyed, turned, and said to the spirit, "I command you in the name of Jesus Christ to come out of her." Then it came out at that moment (see Acts 16:17b–18). Some people from Philippi got angry because of what they had done and had Paul and Silas arrested. "They brought them before the magistrates and said, 'These people are Jews and are disturbing our city and are advocating customs that are not lawful for us Romans to adopt or practice.' The crowd joined in the attack on them, and the magistrates had them stripped and ordered them to be beaten with rods. After inflicting many blows on them, they threw them into prison and instructed the jailer to guard them securely" (Acts 16:20–23).

The last thing we read about Lydia in sacred Scripture is that "when they had come out of the prison, they went to Lydia's house where they saw and encouraged the brothers, and then they left" (Acts 16:40). What peace Paul and his companions must have felt, knowing that when they left the jail, they had a place to stay and regain their physical and spiritual strength before continuing their mission to "proclaim the Word, be persistent whether it is convenient or inconvenient; convince, reprimand, encourage through all patience and teaching" (2 Timothy 4:2).

What does Lydia teach us?

- Never stop praying, since prayer is a loving dialogue between God and humanity. It was precisely when Lydia was praying by the banks of the river that she heard someone speak of Jesus, and thus began her conversion.
- An encounter with Jesus the Christ causes a change in whoever discovers him. Things cannot remain the same after having met the one who is the "Way, the Truth, and the Life" (John 14:6). We see this change in Lydia, who was baptized and opened the doors of her home to the early Christian community.
- Those who truly welcome Jesus and his message of salvation do not remain indifferent but give themselves over to him.
- People can change, just like Paul, who went from being a persecutor of Jesus to being his apostle, calling himself "Paul, an apostle of Christ Jesus by command of God our savior and of Christ Jesus our hope" (1 Timothy 1:1).
- Generosity. Lydia is at the service of God, the kingdom, and everything she has that could be useful at that time.
- Help those who work for God, take care of their material needs, help them financially, and be available to accompany them in their missionary work, encourage them, etc.

- Everyone has something to contribute and establish the kingdom among all people. Lydia was a trader who dedicated herself to selling purple cloth. This made her an independent woman with a profession, and she was surely used to planning, organizing, and formalizing transactions—in short, doing everything a business entailed. These characteristics of her personality would most definitely play a primordial role in her way of acting as an apostle for Christ.
- Lydia teaches us to live the virtue of self-giving to Christ.

What does the *Catechism of the Catholic Church* tell us?

§2472 "The duty of Christians to take part in the life of the Church impels them to act as witnesses of the Gospel and of the obligations that flow from it. This witness is a transmission of the faith in words and deeds. Witness is an act of justice that establishes the truth or makes it known (see Matthew 18:16)."

§442 Saints Peter and Paul profess that Jesus is the Son of God.

§429 Proclaim the kingdom of God.

§849 "The missionary mandate": Go and make disciples of all peoples and baptize them.

§850 "The origin and purpose of mission."

§851 Missionary zeal is inspired by the love of God for all men and women.

§855 "Divisions among Christians" are obstacles to evangelization.

§856 The work of evangelization involves "respectful dialogue with those who do not yet accept the Gospel."

§1490 Conversion is "the movement of return to God."

§2608 "Conversion of heart" is important.

§2612 Following Christ requires vigilance.

Questions for personal reflection

- In what events and circumstances of my life have I given my time, work, and treasures to God?
- Do I know anyone who lives the virtue of self-giving? Someone who gives his or her time, work, and talents to establish the reign of Christ?
- What do I have to give for the establishment of God's reign? What are my talents? What do I consider to be my treasures? How do I use my time?
- Lydia heard Paul's message and converted. Has my life changed since I have gotten to know Jesus in a more personal way?
- Lydia invited Paul and his companions to stay at her house. What do I think of Lydia's invitation to Paul and his companions?
- Lydia accepted the message of salvation that she heard from Paul. Who has spoken to me about Jesus? Has there been anyone who has proclaimed the message of Christ like Saint Paul proclaimed it to Lydia?
- Have I been a Saint Paul for anyone? Have I brought the message of Jesus Christ to others?

Group questions and activities

- What have we learned from Lydia?
- What did we learn from the passages of chapter sixteen of the Acts of the Apostles?
- What have we learned about Paul that we did not know before?
- Read this passage from the Gospel of Matthew below and discuss it:

  "You are the salt of the earth. But if salt loses its taste, with what can it be seasoned? It is no longer good for anything but to be thrown out and trampled underfoot.

You are the light of the world. A city set on a mountain cannot be hidden. Nor do they light a lamp and then put it under a bushel basket; it is set on a lampstand, where it gives light to all in the house. Just so, your light must shine before others, that they may see your good deeds and glorify your heavenly Father."

MATTHEW 5:13–16

- Jesus said, "I am the light of the world. Whoever follows me will not walk in darkness, but will have the light of life" (John 8:12). Give examples of how Jesus and his followers, Christians, are the light of the world.
- Saint Paul tells us in his First Letter to the Corinthians, "So whether you eat or drink, or whatever you do, do everything for the glory of God" (1 Corinthians 10:31). He tells us to do *everything* for the glory of God. What does *everything* mean?

Practical resolutions

- Pray to the Lord to touch my heart like Lydia's.
- Ask God to touch the heart of a family member, a colleague, a neighbor, or a friend who does not know Christ, or who knows him but is far from him.
- Never stop praying, even in hard times, and redouble my efforts at prayer during tough moments.
- Welcome those who work for Christ into my home and make it a place of welcome where everyone is received with kindness.
- Help a priest or a religious sister in their material needs.
- Accept that people can change, as Saint Paul did, and that all is not lost. Give a second or, perhaps, a third chance.
- Put my time, talents, and treasure at the service of the reign of God.

CHAPTER 7

MARY MAGDALENE

First witness of the resurrection

Mary Magdalene meets the Risen One, and as a result overcomes her discouragement and grief at the death of the Master (see John 20:11–18). In his new paschal glory, Jesus tells her to proclaim to the disciples that he has risen: "Go to my brethren" (John 20:17). For this reason, Mary Magdalene could be called "the apostle of the Apostles."

POST–SYNODAL APOSTOLIC EXHORTATION ECCLESIA IN AMERICA
POPE JOHN PAUL II
MEXICO CITY, JANUARY 22, 1999

The resurrection of Christ is our hope! This the Church proclaims today with joy. She announces the hope that is now firm and invincible because God has raised Jesus Christ from the dead. She communicates the hope that she carries in her heart and wishes to share with all people in every place, especially where Christians suffer persecution because of their faith and their commitment to justice and peace. She invokes the hope that can call forth the courage to do good, even when it costs, especially when it costs. Today the Church sings "the day that the Lord has made," and she summons people to joy. [...] Christ, the paschal Victim, the Lamb who has "redeemed the world," the Innocent one who has "reconciled us sinners with the Father." To him, our victorious King, to him who is crucified and risen, we sing out with joy our Alleluia!

Urbi et Orbi Message
Benedict XVI, Easter 2009

He presented himself alive to them by many proofs after he had suffered, appearing to them during forty days and speaking about the kingdom of God.

Acts 1:3

Objective

In this chapter, we will read and study Mary Magdalene and the great event of which she was a witness: the resurrection of Jesus. The Gospel of John tells us:

> On the first day of the week, Mary of Magdala came to the tomb early in the morning, while it was still dark.... But Mary stayed outside the tomb weeping. And as she wept, she bent over into the tomb and saw two angels in white sitting there, one at the head and one at the feet where the body of Jesus had been. And they said to her, "Woman, why are you weeping?" She said to them, "They have taken my Lord, and I don't know where they laid him." When she had said this, she turned around and saw Jesus there, but did not know it was Jesus. Jesus said to her, "Woman, why are you weeping? Whom are you looking for?" She thought it was the gardener and said to him, "Sir, if you carried him away, tell me where you laid him, and I will take him." Jesus said to her, "Mary!" She turned and said to him in Hebrew, "Rabbouni," which means Teacher.
>
> John 20:1, 11–16

What an honor!

Scripture texts: *Matthew 27:56–61; 28:1*
Mark 15:40–47; 16:1–19
Luke 8:2; 24:10
John 19:25; 20:1–18

Introduction to the character

Who was Mary Magdalene?

Mary Magdalene was a woman mentioned by the four evangelists and whom we will read about, study, and delve into in this chapter. Our first goal will be to do her justice, since she has been wrongly identified as a prostitute. If we read the Gospel of Luke carefully, it tells us that Jesus "journeyed from one town and village to another, preaching and proclaiming the good news of the kingdom of God. Accompanying him were the Twelve and some women who had been cured of evil spirits and infirmities, [including] Mary, called Magdalene, from whom seven demons had gone out" (Luke 8:1–2). And if we read the other texts that mention her, none of them says she was a prostitute.

Our second goal is to give her the deference she deserves, since, according to the Gospels, she was the first person to whom Jesus appeared after his resurrection: "When he had risen, early on the first day of the week, he appeared first to Mary Magdalene, out of whom he had driven seven demons" (Mark 16:9).

Our third goal is to remember the greatness, meaning, and importance of being a witness of the resurrection.

Development of the Bible story

As we said earlier, the four evangelists tell us about Mary Magdalene. And they tell us the following:

- She had been possessed by seven demons. Luke says: "Mary, called Magdalene, from whom seven demons had gone out" (Luke 8:2b), as does Mark: "he appeared first to Mary Magdalene, out of whom he had driven seven demons" (Mark 16:9).
- She was one of the women who had accompanied Jesus: Among them were Mary Magdalene and Mary the mother of James and Joseph, and the mother of the sons of Zebedee" (Matthew 27:56; also Mark 15:47 and Luke 8:2).
- She was present during the Passion of Jesus (Mark 15:40).
- She was there at the hour of crucifixion, along with Mary, the Mother of Jesus (John 19:25).
- At the hour of his burial: "Mary Magdalene and Mary the mother of Joses watched where he was laid" (Mark 15:47). Also Matthew 27:61.
- On the first day after Saturday, very early in the morning, she went to the tomb "and saw the stone removed from the tomb. So she ran and went to Simon Peter and to the other disciple whom Jesus loved, and told them, 'They have taken the Lord from the tomb, and we don't know where they put him'" (John 20:1–2).
- She was the first one to whom the risen Jesus appeared (Matthew 28:1–10; Mark 16:9; John 20:14).
- And she was sent by Jesus to make the first proclamation of his resurrection: Mary of Magdala went and announced to the disciples, 'I have seen the Lord,' and what he told her" (John 20:18).

After going over the texts in detail, we can see that not one Gospel quote speaks of Mary Magdalene as a prostitute. What they do say is that she was a follower of Jesus who was ready to be at the foot of the cross and at his burial, and that she was the first person to see the risen Jesus, according to the Gospel narratives.

This is what the Gospels tell us about her. Kind reader, you will most probably wonder where we got the notion that she was a prostitute. We do not have the space in this book to delve into how at a specific time in history people began to think that Mary Magdalene was: the sinful woman who anointed the feet of Jesus in the house of a Pharisee (Luke 7:36–50); Mary the sister of Martha and Lazarus (Luke 10:38–24); and the woman who anointed his feet in Bethany in the house of Simon the leper (Matthew 26:6–16).

Today we have it clear that each one of these Marys is a different person. And we see this clearly reflected in the prayers that the Catholic Church prays on July 22 on the feast of Saint Mary Magdalene. The prayers and readings of that day's liturgical celebration reflect the Church's belief that Mary Magdalene is the woman Jesus chose to be the witness of the resurrection. During the liturgical celebration, the priest recites the Opening Prayer that says:

> "O God, whose Only Begotten Son entrusted Mary Magdalene before all others with announcing the great joy of the resurrection, grant, we pray, that through her intercession and example we may proclaim the living Christ and come to see him reigning in your glory. Who lives and reigns with you in the unity of the Holy Spirit, one God, for ever and ever."

In the first reading at Mass, taken from the Song of Songs, we read: "I found him whom my soul loves" (3:4). The reading from the Gospel is taken from John, chapter 20, which recounts that the Risen Jesus appeared to Mary Magdalene. The text says, "On the first day of the week, Mary of Magdala came to the tomb early in the morning....Jesus said to her, 'Mary!' She turned and said to him in Hebrew, 'Rabbouni,' which means Teacher".... Mary Magdalene went and announced to the disciples, 'I have seen the Lord,' and what he told her" (John 20:1a, 16, 18).

At no time is she mentioned as a reformed prostitute. Thus having clarified who Mary Magdalene was, we return to the essence of this chapter, titled "Mary Magdalene, witness of the resurrection."

To be able to get to the point of the resurrection, we have to remember that Jesus had died on the cross, that he was brought down, wrapped in a burial cloth, and laid in "a rock-hewn tomb in which no one had yet been buried" (Luke 23:53). It was the day of preparation for the Passover. Night was falling and the Sabbath was beginning. The women who had come from Galilee following Jesus had to withdraw, but not before having seen how the body of Jesus was laid in the tomb. "They returned and prepared spices and perfumed oils. Then they rested on the sabbath according to the commandment" (Luke 23:56).

The Gospel of Mark tells us that on the first day after the Sabbath, Mary Magdalene, Mary the mother of James, and Salome went to the tomb of Jesus, bringing perfumes that had been bought to anoint Jesus. And the Gospel of John tells us, "Mary of Magdala came to the tomb...and saw the stone removed from the tomb. So she ran and went to Simon Peter and to the other disciple whom Jesus loved, and told them, 'They have taken the Lord from the tomb, and we don't know where they put him'" (John 20:1–2).

The story continues, telling us how Peter and the other disciple went running toward the tomb, but the other disciple ran faster and arrived first. He looked in and saw the burial cloths on the ground, but did not enter. When Peter arrived, he also saw the burial cloths on the ground, and the cloth that had covered his head, not with the burial cloths, but rolled up in a separate place. "Then the other disciple also went in, the one who had arrived at the tomb first, and he saw and believed. For they did not yet understand the scripture that he had to rise from the dead" (John 20:8–9). Then the two disciples went back home.

Mary, who had stayed outside the tomb crying, looked inside and saw two angels dressed in white, one sitting at the head and the other at the feet of where Jesus' body had been. They asked her why she was crying and whom she was seeking. She answered that she was crying because they had taken her Lord and she did not know where they had put him. She turned around and saw Jesus standing there, but she did not recognize him. Jesus said to her, "Mary!" She turned and said to him in Hebrew, "Rabbouni," which means Teacher. Jesus said to her, "Stop holding on to me, for I have not yet ascended to the Father. But go to my brothers and tell them, 'I am going to my Father and your Father, to my God and your God'" (John 20:16–17). Mary Magdalene went to tell the disciples that she had seen the Lord and what Jesus had told her.

This is Mary Magdalene, the woman we are focusing on in this chapter, a woman who was a faithful follower of Jesus to the end, and who was chosen by Jesus to be a witness of the resurrection before the apostles. She brought the great news that Jesus had conquered death, news that changed the world. Many people have given their lives for a noble cause, to defend their ideals or to fight for justice, but only one has been resurrected; only one has conquered death. That is why the resurrection marks a very important moment for us human beings. By his resurrection, Jesus conquered death so that one day we may rise with him, so that we can live with the hope that there is something more than the here and now, that there is an eternal life where we will find indescribable satisfaction.

"Death is swallowed up in victory. Where, O death, is your victory? Where, O death, is your sting? But thanks be to God who gives us the victory through our Lord Jesus Christ. Therefore, my beloved brothers, be firm, steadfast, always fully devoted to the work of the Lord, knowing that in the Lord your labor is not in vain" (1 Corinthians 15:54b–55; 57–58).

What does Mary Magdalene teach us?

- Even though she had been possessed by seven demons, she was a follower of Jesus. She shows us that we are not bound by our past, that we can change, and that when there is change, there is a future—and if we want it, a future close to Jesus.
- She reveals what it really means to want to be close to Jesus. She went to the tomb in the morning, before the sun had risen, along with the other women who had also walked there to embalm his body.
- She teaches us to be persevering in the quest for Jesus. She wanted to find Jesus at any cost, so first she asked the angels. Then, not giving up, she asked the person she thought was the gardener.
- She shows us how Jesus uses men and women to bear his message. It was Mary Magdalene whom Jesus asked to go and tell the apostles that he has risen, thus making her an *apostle to the apostles.*
- Both the angels and Jesus asked Mary Magdalene why she was crying. Perhaps women are more sensitive to spiritual and emotional realities, or maybe they are socialized differently than men. Regardless, we witness Mary of Magdala here grieving over the loss of Jesus.
- Mary Magdalene helps us visualize her communication with Jesus: When he said her name, she recognized him right away.
- It confirms something we already knew, but that we have to remember: The resurrection is a central part of our faith. The Apostle Paul said so in his First Letter to the Corinthians: "And if Christ has not been raised, then empty too is

our preaching; empty, too, your faith" (1 Corinthians 15:14).

- She reminds us that Jesus reveals himself to us through different people or events.
- Mary Magdalene encourages us to revive our hope of the resurrection, of eternal life.
- She reminds us that we followers of Jesus are not following something, but someone, a risen person, one who has conquered death.

What does the *Catechism of the Catholic Church* tell us?

§638 "The resurrection of Jesus is the crowning truth of our faith in Christ, a faith believed and lived as the central truth by the first Christian community; handed on as fundamental by Tradition; established by the documents of the New Testament; and preached as an essential part of the Paschal mystery along with the cross:
Christ is risen from the dead!
Dying, he conquered death;
To the dead, he has given life (Byzantine Liturgy, Troparion of Easter)."

§641 Christ appears to Mary Magdalene.

§647 Though we celebrate the resurrection, we do not understand it. Yet, we are invited into the mystery of the resurrection.

§651 Confirmation of what Jesus had said and taught.

§652 The resurrection fulfills Christ's promises and those of the Old Testament.

§653 "Jesus' divinity is confirmed by his resurrection."

§654 The resurrection gives us access to a new life through justification and filial adoption.

§655 Christ is the "principle and source of our future resurrection."

Questions for personal reflection

- Do I have an urgent desire to find Jesus, like Mary Magdalene did? Do I do everything I can to meet him as she did?
- Are there circumstances or events of my past life that I feel ashamed about? Have I gone to the sacrament of reconciliation and asked God's forgiveness, knowing that he forgives me and that I have started a new life? If I have not done it, will I? Do I see the need to turn to his mercy and heal the deep wounds that I am carrying?
- Do I look for Jesus? Where? Am I aware that he is present in my daily life, in my family, in my colleagues at work, in the members of my community, but especially in the most needy?
- Do I try to establish communication with Jesus? Do I pray? Am I aware of his presence during the day as I go about my different activities? Do I offer those activities to him? Do I ask for his company and guidance? Do I check with him before making a decision?
- Have I proclaimed Jesus? Have I brought the good news to other people? Am I his apostle?
- Do I think crying is bad or a sign of weakness?
- Do I recognize Jesus in my daily life, and do I see his loving hand in the events of my life?
- What do I think of the resurrection? Do I value the mystery of the resurrection and foresee this promise being fulfilled in my own life?
- Is there anyone who has been a messenger of Jesus for me? Who? How? When?
- Am I excited about getting to heaven? What am I doing to get there?

Group questions and activities

- What have we learned from Mary Magdalene?
- What does Mary Magdalene teach us about following Jesus through good times and bad times?
- Throughout life, who has proclaimed the risen Jesus to us? Parents, grandparents, a religious sister, a teacher, a priest, various friends?
- Jesus gave Mary Magdalene the mission of bringing the news of the resurrection to the apostles. He could have done it himself. Why did he ask her to do it? Why does Jesus use human beings to proclaim his message?
- Why is the resurrection important for humanity? It would be good to consult the *Catechism of the Catholic Church*, which teaches about the resurrection in paragraphs 638–658.
- The virtue of hope is characteristic of the followers of Jesus. Why?
- During the Easter Vigil Mass (the Saturday before resurrection Sunday), a beautiful hymn is recited to recount the prodigious events of salvation history. The hymn is called the *Exsultet* or "Easter Proclamation" and through it, the Church acclaims and rejoices in the resurrection of Jesus. You may read it and discuss it as a group.

Practical resolutions

- Live as a follower of the risen Jesus.
- Give thanks to God for having given us Jesus so that we may have life and have it abundantly (John 10:10).
- Give thanks to Jesus for having died and risen for us, because he was obedient unto death and death on the cross! (Philippians 2:8).
- When the Lenten and Easter season comes around each year, live it differently, aware that it is a time of great joy for us as members of the Church, because Jesus rose again.
- Remember that Jesus uses people to bring us closer to him and that I can be one of those people for others.
- Remember, especially in difficult times, the part of the Easter Proclamation that says:
  "Our birth would have been no gain,
  had we not been redeemed.
  O wonder of your humble care for us!
  O love, O charity beyond all telling,
  To ransom a slave, you gave away your Son!"
- Have hope even when all seems lost, even when it seems there is no way out.
- Remember always that we are Christians (followers of Christ) because we believe in the resurrection.

Prayer

In the Greek Orthodox Church, on the occasion of the Passover of the resurrection, people congratulate each other with the phrase *"Christos Anesti! Alithos Anesti!"* which means "Christ has risen! He has truly risen!"

Now we pray, saying:

Christ, you have truly risen: Be my resurrection and life.
Christ, you have truly risen: Help parents who with sacrifice and self-giving do the best they can to educate their children in the faith.
Christ, you have truly risen: Help workers who daily strive to work honestly.
Christ, you have truly risen: Help those who find no meaning in their lives.
Christ, you have truly risen: Help the homeless and unemployed.
Christ, you have truly risen: Accompany those who are alone, sad, and feeling hopeless.
Christ, you have truly risen: Protect the vulnerable, especially those who cannot defend themselves, such as babies in their mothers' wombs.
Christ, you have truly risen: Be with the prisoners.
Christ, you have truly risen: Protect your priests and consecrated souls.
Christ, you have truly risen: Lead your Church to you.

Christ has risen! He has truly risen!

(Here, encourage each person to finish the following sentences according to whatever intentions he or she carries in his or her heart.)

Christ, you have truly risen: Help…
Christ, you have truly risen: Encourage…
Christ, you have truly risen: Strengthen…
Christ, you have truly risen: Shelter…
Christ, you have truly risen: Welcome…

Christ has risen! He has truly risen!

III.
WOMEN WHO EXPERIENCED THE LOVE AND SALVATION OF JESUS

CHAPTER 8

A woman who suffered from a hemorrhage for twelve years, and her personal encounter with Jesus

[Jesus] went off with him, and a large crowd followed him and pressed upon him. There was a woman afflicted with hemorrhages for twelve years. She had suffered greatly at the hands of many doctors and had spent all that she had. Yet she was not helped but only grew worse. She had heard about Jesus and came up behind him in the crowd and touched his cloak. She said, "If I but touch his clothes, I shall be cured." Immediately her flow of blood dried up. She felt in her body that she was healed of her affliction. Jesus, aware at once that power had gone out from him, turned around in the crowd and asked, "Who has touched my clothes?" But his disciples said to him, "You see how the crowd is pressing upon you, and yet you ask, 'Who touched me?'" And he looked around to see who had done it. The woman, realizing what had happened to her, approached in fear and trembling. She fell down before Jesus and told him the whole truth. He said to her, "Daughter, your faith has saved you. Go in peace and be cured of your affliction."

MARK 5:24–34

Objective

"If I but touch [Jesus'] clothes, I shall be cured" (Mark 5:28), was the desire of this woman who found herself in the crowd surrounding Jesus.

This woman, whom the Gospel tells us had suffered hemorrhages for twelve years, was convinced that if she could touch him, things would change. She took heart and, little by little, got close enough to touch the hem of his garment—and immediately, things did change.

This woman is an example of faith, tenacity, constancy, and effort for us as twenty-first-century Christians. She teaches us to do everything we can to meet Jesus in a personal way.

Scripture texts: *Matthew 9:20–22*
Mark 5:25–34
Luke 8:43–48

Introduction to the character

Who is this woman that the three synoptic Gospels tell us about, and who had suffered hemorrhages for twelve years?

We do not know her name. What we do know is that she was ill and suffering. We know that she had visited many doctors, that she had spent all she had trying to find a cure, that she was unsuccessful, and that she decided to approach Jesus, doing everything she could to touch him.

This woman began by wanting to be healed, and she met Jesus the healer. She began by looking for the gift of health and she met Jesus, the giver of all gifts. It's worth noting that some translations of the Bible call her "the hemorrhaging woman."

Development of the Bible story

The first thing that comes to mind after reading her story is, *Poor woman...twelve years and she couldn't stop the bleeding*! She was probably anemic, pale, sad, tired, and with dark circles under her eyes. But this woman's misfortune did not end there; her tragedy was magnified by the customs of the time. At that time, a woman was considered impure if she had a flow of blood that lasted many days outside of the time of her period. And not only was she considered impure, but in addition, "Any bed on which she lies during such a flow becomes unclean... and any article on which she sits becomes unclean just as during her menstrual period. Anyone who touches them becomes unclean" (Leviticus 15:26–27).

For the past twelve years, this woman had carried not only the physical suffering that comes from a loss of blood, which in general produces weakness and a lack of energy, but during all of that time she had been considered impure and could not live with other people in a normal way. She had been obliged to live in isolation.

The Gospel also tells us that she had spent her entire fortune on visits to doctors, who failed to cure her, while her condition grew worse (see Mark 5:26). What a tragedy this woman's life had become! She was suffering physically, spiritually, financially, and socially.

But her life changed when she met Jesus. The Gospel of Mark tells us that she had heard of Jesus. And that is how many stories of salvation and friendship with the Lord begin—with someone who hears another person speaking about Jesus. Our own relationship with Jesus began that way too, because someone—mom, dad, grandparents, an aunt, a priest, a religious sister, a friend, or colleague—did us the favor and talked to us about Jesus.

Let us continue with the story of this woman. The Gospel tells us that when the people saw Jesus healing many, all those who suffered any kind of ailment pressed in on him to touch him. And this woman also decided to draw close to him. We imagine that getting close to Jesus in those days was not so easy, since he was surrounded by all those who wanted to be healed.

But she shows her determination and daring: She had to touch Jesus and she got right to it. She began making her way through the crowd, "came up behind him, and touched the tassel on his cloak" (Matthew 9:20) with the hope that she could be healed just by touching his clothing. To understand exactly why she wanted to touch the tassel on his cloak, we have to mention what the Book of Numbers says: "Speak to the Israelites and tell them that throughout their generations they are to make tassels for the corners of their garments [...]. The sight of the cord will remind you of all the commandments of the LORD and you will do them, without prostituting yourself going after the desires of your hearts and your eyes. Thus you will remember to do all my commandments and you will be holy to your God. [...] I, the LORD, am your God" (Numbers 15:38–41). The tassels on the corner of the garment served as a reminder for the Israelites that fulfilling the Lord's commandments would make them holy before God.

What a beautiful image of the woman doing everything in her power to get close to Jesus. And she was immediately cured! Jesus noticed "that power had gone out from him, turned around in the crowd and asked, 'Who has touched my clothes?' But his disciples said to him, 'You see how the crowd is pressing upon you, and yet you ask, "Who touched me?"'" (Matthew 5:30–31). "Someone has touched me; for I know that power has gone out from me" (Luke 8:46). And he looked around to see who had touched him. "When the woman realized that she had not escaped notice, she came forward trembling. Falling down before him, she explained in the presence of all the people why she had touched him and how she had been healed immediately" (Luke 8:47).

Jesus said to her, "Daughter, your faith has saved you; go in peace" (Luke 8:48). "Your faith has saved you"—what beautiful and wonderful words spoken by Jesus to a woman who had suffered for twelve years from physical illness and emotional isolation.

This is an extraordinary salvation story, a story that shows us what faith does: It teaches us the difference between hearing someone speak of Jesus and having a personal relationship with him, between merely wanting something and applying all the means necessary to achieve it. In short, it is a wonderful story of faith.

What does the story of this woman who suffered twelve years of hemorrhages teach us?

- She teaches us what faith achieves. Jesus clearly told her, "Daughter, your faith has saved you. Go...and be cured of your affliction" (Mark 5:34).
- She gives us courage to take the initiative, not to settle just for having the wish, the eagerness, the desire to come closer to Jesus, but to be proactive.
- To come closer to Jesus, we have to do our part.
- To be able to "touch" Jesus, we have to dedicate time to him.
- Jesus gives special attention to those who suffer.
- To look for a personal encounter with Jesus.
- We can do great good for others when we talk to them about Jesus.
- Sometimes we have to take a risk to get what we want.
- Jesus is attentive to us and to our physical and spiritual needs.
- Don't look down on people who suffer physical deformations just because they are different or are going through a tough time.

- It is unfair to "label" or classify people. If we say "they are like this or that," our own label limits them in our minds, since from then onward they can only be that and nothing else. This attitude is truly cruel and unjust.
- In short, the story teaches us to have faith, to do our part to meet Jesus in a personal way.
- Finally, it shows us how the ones who win when they "touch" Jesus are all of us, human beings.

What does the *Catechism of the Catholic Church* tell us?

§2616 "Prayer to Jesus is answered by him already during his ministry, through signs that anticipate the power of his death and resurrection: Jesus hears the prayer of faith, expressed in words (the leper [see Mark 1:40–41], Jairus [see Mark 5:36], the Canaanite woman [see Mark 7:29], the good thief [see Luke 23:39–43]), or in silence (the bearers of the paralytic [see Mark 2:5], the woman with a hemorrhage who touches his clothes [see Mark 5:28], the tears and ointment of the sinful woman [see Luke 7:37–38])."

§146 The definition of faith given in the Letter to the Hebrews: "Faith is the assurance of things hoped for, the conviction of things not seen" (Hebrews 11:1).

§547 "Jesus accompanies his words with many 'mighty works, wonders, and signs'."

§548 Jesus grants the faithful what they ask of him.

§549 Jesus did not come to abolish all earthly evils, but to free humanity from sin: "the greatest slavery."

§561 "The whole of Christ's life was a continual teaching: his silences, his miracles, his gestures, his prayer...his special affection for the little and the poor...."

§1718 Jesus helps us to order our lives by teaching us the Beatitudes, corresponding to our innate desire for happiness.

§1731 Freedom gives us "the power, rooted in reason and free will, to act or not to act."

§1733 "The more one does what is good, the freer one becomes," since freedom is ordered to what is good.

§1735 "Responsibility for an action can be diminished or even nullified by ignorance, duress...and other psychological or social factors."

Questions for personal reflection

- What do I think about this woman's behavior?
- Would I be capable of going into the crowd, exposing myself to being mistreated so as to have a personal encounter with Jesus?
- Have I had the experience of meeting Jesus personally? Is Jesus something more to me than just a holy card with his picture on it? Is he my life's companion?
- Most people would have treated this woman like someone of little importance or as an annoyance. How would I have treated her? Would I have come close to her even though she was considered impure? Or would I have kept my distance? Would I have criticized her for mixing with the people when she knew that the law said she should not do it?
- What did I learn from Jesus' answer to the woman? How does Jesus treat those who suffer? How do I treat them?
- Have I ever been in touch with someone who was going through great or excruciating suffering? How did I treat that person? How do I wish I had treated him or her?
- Have I suffered much? How did others treat me? How have I treated Jesus?
- What can I do to "touch" Jesus? Am I ready to "touch" Jesus even though this will require an effort on my part?
- Am I constant in my resolutions, or do I leave things unfinished when difficulties come up?

Group questions and activities

- What have we learned from this woman who suffered a flow of blood for twelve years?
- We not only touch his cloak, but we have the sacraments. Have we come to understand that we touch Jesus in the sacraments more profoundly than if we were to merely touch his cloak?
- Share what you think about the definition of faith in the Letter to the Hebrews: "Faith is the assurance of things hoped for, the conviction of things not seen" (Hebrews 11:1).
- What does this verse from the Book of Sirach teach us? "My son, when you are ill, do not delay, but pray to God, for it is he who heals" (Sirach 38:9).
- Jesus does not miss a soul among the crowd. Although he was surrounded by people who were pressing in on him, Jesus knew perfectly well that the hemorrhaging woman had touched him. Share some occasions when you have felt the presence of Jesus in your lives.
- In his encyclical letter *Deus Caritas Est*, Pope Benedict XVI writes, "Being Christian is not the result of an ethical choice or a lofty idea, but the encounter with...a person [Christ], who gives life a new horizon" (*Deus Carita Est*, 1). What do you think of this statement?
- The world divides people between the important and the unimportant. For Jesus, we are all important; we are all children of God. Do we really believe this? Does it comfort us to know it?
- In his Second Letter to the Corinthians, Paul tells us that Jesus said, "My grace is enough for you" (2 Corinthians 12:9). Does it comfort us to know that we have his help?
- Comment on how this statement of Jesus' makes you feel: "Come to me, all you who labor and are burdened, and I will give you rest. Take my yoke upon you and learn from me,

for I am meek and humble of heart; and you will find rest for your selves. For my yoke is easy, and my burden light" (Matthew 11:28–30).

- Read the following quote from the Book of Sirach and share your opinion about what it says: "Make friends with the doctor, for he is essential to you; God has also established him in his profession. He endows people with knowledge, to glory in his mighty works, through which the doctor eases pain, and the druggist prepares his medicines. Thus God's work continues without cease in its efficacy on the surface of the earth." (Sirach 38:1, 6–8).

Practical resolutions

- Ask God to increase my faith.
- Ask Jesus to allow me to have a personal encounter with him.
- Dedicate time to prayer, to reading sacred Scripture, to reading books that bring me closer to Jesus.
- Speak about Jesus to others to bring them closer to him.
- Ask Jesus to touch the heart of a family member, a colleague at work, a neighbor, a friend who does not know him or who knows him but is far from him.
- Receive the sacraments, especially the Eucharist and reconciliation.
- When facing suffering, do what this woman did: Run to Jesus and do whatever I can to be close to him.
- Help others persevere through moments of difficulty and physical and emotional trials.
- Treat people as what they are: creatures of God. Do this regardless of the color of their skin, their country of origin, the language they speak, or their educational background.
- Don't "label" people by external appearances.
- Be constant in what I do. If I start something, finish it.

Prayer

Prayer of Pope John Paul II at Nirmal Hrinday, a place of loving care for the sick and dying run by Mother Teresa, Calcutta (India), February 3, 1986:

All-powerful and ever-living God,
Father of the poor,
Comfort of the sick,
Hope of the dying,
Your love guides every moment of our lives.

[...] In this place of loving care for the sick and dying,
we lift our minds and hearts to you in prayer.
We praise you for the gift of human life
and especially for the promise of everlasting life.
We know that you are always near
to the broken-hearted and the destitute,
and to all the weak and suffering.

O God of tenderness and compassion,
Accept the prayers we offer
for our sick brothers and sisters.
Increase their faith and trust in you.
Comfort them with your loving presence and,
if it be your will, restore their health,
give them renewed strength of body and soul.

O loving Father,
bless those who are dying,
bless all those who will soon meet you face to face.
We believe that you have made death the gateway to eternal life.
Keep our dying brothers and sisters in your love,
and bring them safely home to eternal life with you.

O God, the Source of all strength,
watch over and protect those who care for the sick
and assist the dying.
Give them a courageous and gentle spirit.
Sustain them in their efforts to bring comfort and healing.
Make them ever more a radiant sign of your transforming love.

O Lord of life and Foundation of our hope,
pour out your abundant blessings upon all who live and work
and die [...].
Fill them with your peace and grace.
Let them see that you are a loving Father,
a God of mercy and compassion. Amen.

CHAPTER 9

THE SAMARITAN WOMAN

A woman whose heart was converted and who became a follower of Jesus

"Yes, God thirsts for our faith and our love. As a good and merciful father, he wants our total, possible good, and this good is he himself. The Samaritan woman, on the other hand, represents the existential dissatisfaction of one who does not find what she seeks. She had five husbands and now she lives with another man; her going to and from the well to draw water expresses a repetitive and resigned life. However, everything changes for her that day, thanks to the conversation with the Lord Jesus, who upsets her to the point that she leaves her pitcher of water and runs to tell the villagers: 'Come, see a man who told me all that I ever did. Can this be the Christ?' (John 4:29). Dear brothers and sisters, like the Samaritan woman, let us also open our hearts to listen trustingly to God's Word in order to encounter Jesus who reveals his love to us and tells us: 'I who speak to you am he' (John 4:26)."

BENEDICT XVI
ANGELUS, THIRD SUNDAY OF LENT,
FEBRUARY 24, 2008

Objective

"If you knew the gift of God and who is saying to you, 'Give me a drink,' you would have asked him and he would have given you living water" (John 4:10). With these words, a beautiful story of conversion and communication begins.

Scripture text: *John 4:4–42*

Introduction to the character

In this chapter, we will talk about an encounter between Jesus and a woman at the well of Jacob, situated in the region of Samaria. It was a very fruitful encounter, since Jesus spoke to her of "living water," showed her that he knew her life, and revealed that he was the Messiah.

What seems like a chance encounter becomes a process of conversion that ends with the propagation of the Messianic identity of Jesus, since the Samaritan woman runs to bring the news to the inhabitants of the city, telling them that she had met the Messiah. The townspeople made a beautiful and conclusive declaration of faith at the end of the narration: "We know that this is truly the savior of the world" (John 4:42).

Development of the Bible story

First of all, to be able to understand this Gospel passage well, we have to explain where Samaria was located. In Jesus' time, the geographical area where he preached was divided into three territories. In the north was Galilee, where the cities of Nazareth, Capernaum, Cana, and Tiberias were located. In the extreme south was the territory of Judea, where the cities of Jerusalem and Bethlehem were found. And between these two territories was Samaria.

It should be clarified that there was a longstanding enmity between the Jews and the Samaritans. It was a quarrel that began in the time of the reconstruction of the Temple of Jerusalem (Ezra 4). So the Samaritan woman was surprised at Jesus' request for water, and asked him, "How can you, a Jew, ask me, a Samaritan woman, for a drink? (For Jews [used] nothing in common with Samaritans)" (John 4:9).

How did Jesus get to the region of Samaria when he could have taken another road to get from Judea to Galilee? Did he perhaps want to meet this Samaritan woman? Did he need to meet with her? Did he need her to convert? Most certainly yes, since Jesus did not miss the chance to get in touch with those who needed him.

Let us recall other occasions when Jesus "met" those who needed him, like when he arrived in Jericho, "looked up and said to him, 'Zacchaeus, come down quickly, for today I must stay at your house'" (Luke 19:5). There was also the time when he went to Peter's house and "met" Peter's mother-in-law, "lying in bed with a fever. He touched her hand, [and] the fever left her" (Matthew 8:14b–15).

The Gospel of John is the only one of the four Gospels that tells us about this meeting with the Samaritan woman. It tells us that Jesus, tired from the journey, sat by the edge of the well at the time we call midday, the time when the sun is hottest and the heat is raging. Then he struck up a conversation with the woman.

Some might wonder: What was this woman doing going to the well when the sun was at its height? We do not know for sure, but some experts say that she was surely trying to avoid coming into contact with the other women of the town who went for water early in the morning or in the evening, when the sun was less strong. Why did she want to avoid contact with them? We shall see that further on.

Jesus asks her to give him a drink (John 4:7), since his disciples had gone to the city to buy food. A bit puzzled by the request, the woman reminds him that Jews and Samaritans are not on speaking terms.

Jesus answers in a masterful way, in what we can consider the central verse of this story: "If you knew the gift of God and who is saying to you, 'Give me a drink,' you would have asked him and he would have given you living water" (John 4:10). Jesus wants to communicate his love. He wants her to know how much he loves her, how attentive he is to her. He tells her and he tells us that if only we understood who he is, we would be the ones asking him for his "living water" and he would give it to us.

The woman asks him how he will do that if he has nothing with which to draw water from the well, which is very deep. Jesus answers, "Everyone who drinks this water will be thirsty again; but whoever drinks the water I shall give will never thirst; the water I shall give will become in him a spring of water welling up to eternal life" (John 4:13–14). Naturally, the woman asks for that water so that she will not have to thirst again.

And so Jesus came into contact with this woman to quench her thirst, which was not just a physical thirst. It was rather a deeper thirst, a thirst for God, although she did not understand it yet.

The story continues with Jesus asking her to call her husband. She confesses that she does not have one, to which Jesus answers that she is speaking truthfully, because the man she is with at that moment is not her husband, and she has had five others besides. Now we understand why she went to the well at midday! It was to avoid meeting the wives of those men!

Embarrassed, the Samaritan woman answers, "Sir, I can see that you are a prophet" (John 4:19).

The conversation continues with Jesus speaking to her about God. He tells her that God is Spirit, and that he must be worshiped in spirit and in truth (John 4:24). The woman tells him that she knows the Messiah is coming, and that when he does, he will explain everything. To this, Jesus answers, "I am he, the one who is speaking with you" (John 4:26).

With this revelation, the woman feels compelled to proclaim to the townspeople that she has found the Messiah. And leaving her water jar, she runs to the city and tells the people. "'Come see a man who told me everything I have done. Could he possibly be the Messiah?' They went out of the town and came to him" (John 4:29–30).

Meanwhile, the disciples have arrived with food they bought, and they insist that Jesus eat. Jesus answers, "My food is to do the will of the one who sent me and to finish his work" (John 4:34).

In this passage, we see how Jesus was totally committed and focused on his mission. Jesus speaks of the water that gives life; the woman speaks of the water that quenches thirst. The same happens with the apostles. Jesus speaks of his food, which is to do the will of his Father, and the disciples are speaking about the food that satiates hunger. Each one has his concerns; each one has his loves.

The meeting that Jesus has with the Samaritan woman turns her into a messenger. Her conversion leads her to speak to others about the treasure she has found. Anyone who meets God cannot stay silent. The truth is so great that one wants to share it with others. That is how many of the Samaritans of that town began to believe in him.

"When the Samaritans came to him, they invited him to stay with them; and he stayed there two days. Many more began to believe in him because of his word, and they said to the woman, 'We no longer believe because of your word; for we have heard for ourselves, and we know that this is truly the savior of the world'" (John 4:40–42).

What do we learn from the story of this Samaritan woman whose heart was converted and who became a follower of Jesus?

- She teaches us that Jesus wants us to know the gift of God.
- The Samaritan woman reminds us that Jesus can give us living water, which "will become in [us] a spring of water welling up to eternal life" (John 4:14).
- It teaches us that Jesus, as a true man, needed to drink water, grew tired on the journey, and sat down to rest.
- It reminds us that Jesus is true God and true man, and thus he understands us. He understands our tiredness, our fatigue, our sorrows and joys.
- She teaches us that someone who meets Jesus cannot remain silent. That person becomes a herald of the Gospel, of the Good News.
- It shows us how Christian life is based on two pillars: conversion and communication. Conversion is brought to its plenitude when it is shared with others.
- It shows us how the Samaritan was, without a doubt, a woman others considerd inferior, not just because of where she lived but also because of her lifestyle. Yet Jesus reached her and sat at the well where she usually came so that he could talk to her.
- It reminds us that for Jesus, there are no second-class citizens. He came to save everyone. He tells us, "Those who are healthy do not need a physician, but the sick do" (Luke 5:31).
- That the love God has for us is like "a spring of water welling up to eternal life" (John 4:14).

- That people may have major problems and be far from God, but once they come close to God they are so full of gratitude and wonder that their feeling of shame dies and they become a spokesperson for the truth. The Samaritan woman gave a clear message to others: *Look at what I was, and look at what I am after meeting Jesus.*
- It shows us how the Samaritans, whom this woman told about Jesus, did not settle for a faith received secondhand but ran to meet Jesus themselves.
- We learn how the woman went from a superficial search to a deeper quest, from seeing Jesus as a mere Jewish man to seeing him as the Messiah, from wanting water to quenching her thirst, and finally rejoicing in the "living water."
- She shows us how her faith and desire to share Jesus inspires her to leave her water jar that she had come to fill and run to tell others that she had met the Savior of the world.
- We also learn that human things and loves are not everything, since we were made for eternity, and only God can quench that thirst.
- It teaches us that with her testimony, this woman got many others to know Jesus, who went to him looking for "living water" to quench spiritual thirst.
- It shows us how this woman became a messenger and apostle for the townspeople.
- It clarifies that the Samaritan woman had been waiting for the coming of the Messiah, trusting that he would teach them everything.
- In short, it teaches us that Jesus took the first step in this woman's conversion, but she had to take the next steps, since God respects our freedom.

What does the *Catechism of the Catholic Church* tell us?

§1435 "Conversion is accomplished in daily life by gestures of reconciliation, concern for the poor, the exercise and defense of justice and right (Isaiah 1:17), by the admission of faults to one's brethren, fraternal correction, revision of life, examination of conscience, spiritual direction, acceptance of suffering, endurance of persecution for the sake of righteousness. Taking up one's cross each day and following Jesus is the surest way of penance (Luke 9:23)."

§160 Christ invites us to faith and conversion, but he does not force us.

§981 After the resurrection, Jesus sent his apostles and disciples to preach conversion for the forgiveness of sins.

§1036 The teachings of the Church about hell are a call to conversion.

§1423 The sacrament of penance, or reconciliation, is a "sacrament of conversion."

§1428 "Christ's call to conversion continues to resound in the life of Christians."

§1430 Conversion of heart is intimately tied to contrition.

§1432 God restores our life and graces us to change our hearts.

§1440 Sin breaks our communion with God and the people of God (the Church); thus, we are healed through the sacrament of penance.

§1502 Sickness is a path of conversion.

§1848 "Grace must uncover the sin to convert our hearts."

§1888 Interior conversion leads to social changes for the good of humanity, as we are inspired to serve Christ through others.

§1896 Conversion of heart creates in us a desire to seek justice.
§1989 "The first work of the grace of the Holy Spirit is *conversion*."
§2560 "The wonder of prayer is revealed" little by little to those who pray.
§2595 Prophets call us to conversion.
§2652 "The Holy Spirit is the 'living water'."

Questions for personal reflection

- What did I learn from the Samaritan woman?
- Would I be capable of recognizing Jesus as she did?
- How did I meet Jesus?
- Did someone speak to me about Jesus?
- What convinced me? The words of the person who spoke to me about Jesus or how he or she lived?
- Do I give witness to Jesus with my life?
- Jesus said to them, "My food is to do the will of the one who sent me and to finish his work" (John 4:34). What is my food?
- Do I set time aside for prayer where the Lord gives me "living water" to drink and feeds me?
- Do I believe that Jesus is the Messiah, the savior of the world, the one who has "living water?" If I truly believe it, do I live like a believer?
- What am I thirsty for? What am I lacking to be totally happy?
- Do I feel the urgency of the Samaritan to proclaim Jesus to others?
- Have I spoken to anyone about Jesus?

Group questions and activities

- Below we present various quotes from sacred Scripture that speak about water in a figurative sense. They speak to me about the soul's thirst for God and of the water that only God gives. Read and discuss which of these you like best, and also which one speaks more of God and of how God acts.

    - "As the deer longs for streams of water, so my soul longs for you, O God" (Psalm 42:2).
    - "All you who are thirsty, come to the water!" (Isaiah 55:1).
    - "On that day, fresh water will flow from Jerusalem, half to the eastern sea, and half to the western sea" (Zechariah 14:8).
    - "Two evils my people have done: they have forsaken me, the source of living waters; They have dug themselves cisterns, broken cisterns that cannot hold water" (Jeremiah 2:13).
    - "To the thirsty I will give a gift from the spring of life-giving water" (Revelation 21:6).
    - "I will pour out water upon the thirsty ground, streams upon the dry land; I will pour out my spirit upon your offspring, my blessing upon your descendants" (Isaiah 44:3).
    - "For the Lamb who is in the center of the throne will shepherd them and lead them to springs of life-giving water, and God will wipe away every tear from their eyes" (Revelation 7:17).
    - "With joy you will draw water from the fountains of salvation" (Isaiah 12:3).

- Compose a prayer of petition with the refrain: "[Lord], give me this water, so that I may not be thirsty" (John 4:15).
- In a general audience, Pope John Paul II spoke about the Samaritan woman and how to transmit faith in Jesus. Carefully read and comment on this passage:

"Woman has a special aptitude to transmit the faith, and for this reason, Jesus turns to her for evangelization. That is what happened with the Samaritan woman, whom Jesus met at the well of Jacob and whom he chose for the first diffusion of the new faith in non-Jewish territory. The evangelist notes that, after having personally accepted faith in Christ, the Samaritan woman hurried to share that faith with others."

John Paul II
General Audience
July 13, 1994

Practical resolutions

- Live with the peace of knowing that Jesus can give me living water to drink that will be a fountain welling up to eternal life.
- Learn from Jesus who, although he had a lot to do, took time to rest by the side of the well and talk with the Samaritan woman.
- Learn from the Samaritan woman to speak to others about that personal encounter with Jesus.
- Live in such a way that my actions, my generosity, and my joy show my conversion, following the advice of Saint Francis of Assisi: "Preach the Gospel always. Use words when necessary."
- Always to be available to everyone, as Jesus was.
- Give our material and spiritual help to those who need it, remembering Jesus' words: "Whatever you did for one of these least brothers of mine, you did for me" (Matthew 25:40).
- Leave my "water jars," my securities, my material attachments to proclaim Jesus to others.

Prayer

Lord Jesus, you who know human hearts to perfection,
Because you not only created them but had one when you became man.
You know better than anyone what I have in my heart.
You know my past, all that I have lived through these years of life that you have given me.
You know my present, and you know what I am going through now.
You know my sorrows, my limitations, my desires, my joys, and my hopes.
That is why I turn today to you, Jesus.
I am like the Samaritan woman, with a water jar that I always want to fill.
Nothing satisfies me, because there is nothing created that can quench my thirst for you.
I beg you to come into my life, to penetrate my heart in depth,
And to take out everything that separates me from you.
Help me to be yours, to be totally clean, so that you can fill my water jar with you.
And may you always be in me.
I ask you to imbue in my heart a generous response to the needs of my brothers and sisters, all people.
I ask you to help me realize that the path of the Gospel is the only path to follow to be happy always and to fulfill myself as a child of the heavenly Father.
I pray that I, like the Samaritan woman, will be capable of leaving everything I am attached to and go running to share you with others.
Amen.

CHAPTER 10

The faith and perseverance of a non-Jewish woman

"The liturgy presents a rare example of faith to us: a Canaanite woman who asks Jesus to heal her daughter who was 'terribly troubled by a demon.' The Lord resisted her insistent entreaties and seemed impervious to them even when the disciples themselves interceded for her, as the Evangelist Matthew relates. In the end, however, confronted by the perseverance and humility of this unknown woman, Jesus consented: 'Woman, you have great faith! Your wish will come to pass' (see Matthew 15: 21–28). 'Woman, you have great faith!' Jesus singles out this humble woman as an example of indomitable faith. Her insistence in imploring Christ's intervention is an encouragement to us never to lose heart and not to despair, even in the harshest trials of life. The Lord does not close his eyes to the needs of his children, and if he seems at times insensitive to their requests, it is only in order to test them and to temper their faith."

POPE BENEDICT XVI
ANGELUS
AUGUST 14, 2005

Objective

If living virtuously is good, persevering in living virtuously is better.

That is the case of this woman, who lived the theological virtue of faith and the virtue of perseverance. By faith, she believed in Jesus and put her trust in him. By the virtue of perseverance, she did everything possible to achieve what she proposed. And she did all this without losing her good spirit, in spite of being questioned by Jesus.

At the end, this woman achieved her objective: the healing of her daughter.

Scripture texts: *Matthew 15:21–28*
Mark 7:24–30

Introduction to the character

Jesus goes with his disciples to the region of Tyre and Sidon, located at the northeast of the region of Galilee. There was a woman who lived in this region and begged Jesus to cure her daughter, who was tormented by a demon. So persistent was her plea that even the disciples interceded for her, just to make her be quiet.

The woman persevered in her petition, overcoming Jesus' refusal with her arguments. The story ends with the healing of her daughter and Jesus' beautiful words: "O woman, great is your faith! Let it be done for you as you wish" (Matthew 15:28).

Development of the Bible story

This is an extraordinary story about the faith and perseverance of a woman who was not a member of the Jewish people and whose persistence got Jesus to cure her daughter.

Matthew calls her the Canaanite woman because of the Old Testament name for the region where she lived. Mark calls her the Syro-Phoenician woman because of her origin, and tells us that she was a pagan, that she did not worship Yahweh, the God of the Jewish people.

This woman begs Jesus, screaming, "Have pity on me, Lord, Son of David! My daughter is tormented by a demon" (Matthew 15:22). This woman must surely have heard about Jesus and the miracles he had worked, of the cures he had done, and some even speculated that he could be the Messiah long awaited by the Jews. She must have thought, *This is my chance to get a person of this caliber to cure my daughter who is possessed by a demon.*

So persistent was her plea that the disciples begged Jesus to grant what she asked, just so that she would leave them in peace. In response, he answered, "I was sent only to the lost sheep of the house of Israel" (Matthew 15:24). Jesus wanted to emphasize that his mission was first to gather all of the faithful of the people of Israel, whom we also call the Jewish people. Thus, it was of primary importance to change the hearts of the members of the Jewish people so that they would then be "a light to the nations, that my salvation may reach to the ends of the earth" (Isaiah 49:6).

But the woman kept going, and when Jesus refused, she continued insisting. Kneeling, she begged him, "Lord, help me" (Matthew 15:25b)." Jesus answered her, "It is not right to take the food of the children and throw it to the dogs" (Matthew 15:26). To the men and women of the twenty-first century, this answer from Jesus sounds very harsh. To understand the reason for his words, we enter the mindset of those who existed in Jesus' time.

The name "Canaanite," which Jesus uses to describe this woman, has its origin in the ancient rivalry between the Jewish people and their neighbors in the land of Canaan, considered pagans because they did not worship Yahweh. And the Jews referred to the pagans as "dogs." Saying that it was not good to take the food of the children and throw it to the dogs meant that it was not good to give to the pagans what belonged first of all to the Jewish people.

To this, the woman answers, “Please, Lord, for even the dogs eat the scraps that fall from the table of their masters” (Matthew 15:27). She humbly recognizes that the messianic promises were reserved for the Jewish people, yet she continues insisting that he give her something, even though it is bread crumbs in comparison to the full promise. “Then Jesus said to her in reply, ‘O woman, great is your faith! Let it be done for you as you wish.’ And her daughter was healed from that hour” (Matthew 15:28).

What does this story about the faith and perseverance of the non-Jewish woman teach us?

- It tells us how Jesus says the words we all want to hear: that we are loved, that someone sees and appreciates our inner beauty, and that we are not alone when we have to face our difficulties and problems.
- It reminds us that prayer must come from a humble heart, that it does not seek to impose its own way on what God does. Rather, the humble heart knows it is little before Jesus and unworthy of receiving his help. But even in that humility, it trusts in the mercy of God.
- It shows us a woman who trusts totally in Jesus.
- She shows us how to put our trust and hope in God, who knows how to draw “good” out of what are apparently “evils.”
- It reminds us of Jesus’ words about prayer: “Ask and it will be given to you; seek and you will find; knock and the door will be opened to you” (Matthew 7:7).
- She sets an example of patience and the importance of persevering in prayer. Our time is not God’s time. The prophet Habukkuk tells us, “For the vision is a witness for the ap-

pointed time, a testimony to the end; it will not disappoint. If it delays, wait for it, it will surely come, it will not be late" (Habukkuk 2:3).

- This woman's attitude shows us how people pray when they believe in Jesus.
- Prayer must be sustained by faith in Jesus and in absolute trust in him.
- She teaches us prayer and reverence by kneeling before Jesus. This allows us to see how she recognizes Jesus as someone before whom it was worthwhile to kneel.
- This sets an example of a parent's love and what it is capable of doing.
- It teaches us the greatness and importance of perseverance. This woman got her daughter cured because she persevered in prayer.
- It shows us how she conquered shame, the fear of what others will say, and cowardice, because she was convinced that it was worthwhile to insist that Jesus cure her daughter.
- She did not despair, give up, or get upset, although she was intruding. She intruded so much that the disciples came to tell Jesus to help her because she was screaming after them.
- It teaches us what hope and perseverance are all about. Although Jesus told her that he came first to the members of the house of Israel and she was a Syro-Phoenician woman, she persevered for the good of her daughter.
- It illustrates this woman's great faith. We see how Jesus praises her for her faith.
- We learn of the mother and daughter's affliction.
- It shows us a true exchange of words, feelings, and ideas between Jesus and the woman. We can see that this was truly an encounter between two people in which each one had clear objectives.
- We see how Jesus talks to people in a natural way, since he is true God and true man.

What does the *Catechism of the Catholic Church* tell us?

Perseverance

§2742 Persevere in virtue: faith, hope, and love.

Faith

§151 Belief in Jesus, the Son of God.
§154 "Faith is an authentically human act."
§155 "In faith, the intellect and will cooperate with divine grace."
§158 Faith tries to understand.
§161 Faith is needed.
§166 "Faith is...the free response of the human person to the initiative of God."
§179 "Faith is a supernatural gift from God."
§180 Believing is a free and conscious act.
§2113 Idolatry, the worship or interest in false gods, is a "constant temptation to faith."

Trust

§305 God takes care of the smallest needs of his children.
§310 "With infinite wisdom and goodness God freely willed to create a world 'in a state of journeying' towards its ultimate perfection."
§2547 The Lord laments that the rich put their trust in their goods.
§2756 "Filial trust is put to the test when we feel that our prayer" is not being heard.
§2828 The trust of children who expect all good things from the Father: "Give us this day our daily bread."
§2836 Trust "this day."

Questions for personal reflection

- What do I think of the behavior of this non-Jewish woman?
- Would I be capable of doing what she did? Would I be embarrassed?
- What did I learn from the dialogue between Jesus and this woman?
- Have I ever found myself in a similar situation in which I ask and ask, and it seems that Jesus is not listening to me? When and how was it? What happened at the end?
- When someone needy asks for my help, how do I respond? Like Jesus or like the disciples?
- How do I respond to those whom I don't like, who bother me, who test my patience?
- How do I respond to people who constantly require my attention, who constantly want me to do things for them? Do I get exasperated?
- How persistent, constant, and tireless am I in what I set out to do?
- How persistent, constant, and tireless am I in prayer? Do I give up easily?
- Have I asked Jesus to teach me to pray like one of his disciples did: "Lord, teach us to pray" (Luke 11:1).

Group questions and activities

- What do you think of this woman's way of acting?
- What do you think about how Jesus acted?
- What is the difference between the way the disciples reacted to this woman and the way Jesus reacted?
- What did Saint Teresa of Ávila mean when she said, "Humility is truth?"

- Saint Paul wrote to the inhabitants of Philippi, "Because of this, God greatly exalted him and bestowed on him the name that is above every name, that at the name of Jesus every knee should bend, of those in heaven and on earth and under the earth, and every tongue confess that Jesus Christ is Lord, to the glory of God the Father (Philippians 2:9–11).
- What does Paul mean when he says, "that at the name of Jesus every knee should bend, of those in heaven and on earth" (Philippians 2:10)?
- This woman told Jesus, "Have pity on me, Lord, Son of David! My daughter is tormented by a demon" (Matthew 15:22).
- Who is suffering? The mother, the daughter, or both? Why?
- What is humility? Look it up in the dictionary, on the Internet, and compare the different definitions. According to these definitions, why do we say that this woman was humble?
- This is an encounter between Jesus and the woman. Did both get their wish?
- In his homily at the prayer vigil with the youth at World Youth Day in Madrid in 2011, Pope Benedict XVI said, "Dear friends, may no adversity paralyze you. Do not be afraid of the world or the future or your weaknesses."
    - Does this quote encourage us?
    - Why does he say not to be afraid?
- Psalm 91 wants us to understand that God takes very great care of us. Verses 3 and 4 say, "He will rescue you from the fowler's snare, from the destroying plague, He will shelter you with his pinions, and under his wings you may take refuge."
- What do you feel when you hear these words?
- Do they give you comfort, security, consolation?

Practical resolutions

- I will seek to dedicate time to prayer. It would be good to set a time and find a suitable place for it.
- When someone comes to me looking for my help, looking to be heard, looking to feel loved, I will remember this story from the Gospel.
- I will help someone who has a sick family member.
- Whenever I can, I will tell people that I appreciate their goodness of heart and their efforts to do good.
- I will ask God to help me remember that he is the Creator, I am his creature, and that he protects me.
- I will apply all the means necessary to persevere in my resolutions.
- When I enter a church, I will kneel down with full respect before the tabernacle.
- When I have the opportunity to do a good deed but I am stopped by the fear of what others will say or am feeling embarrassed, I will remember this woman and her courage.
- I will make my prayer an exchange of love with Jesus.
- I will remember Saint Teresa of Ávila's words about humility.

Prayer

Fifteen minutes in the presence of Jesus in the Blessed Sacrament

"It is not necessary, my child, to know a lot to please me
greatly; it is enough for you to love me fervently.
Speak to me simply here, as you would speak to your
mother or your brother. Do you need to pray to me as
a favor to someone else? Tell me the person's name,
whether it is your parents, your brothers and sisters and
friends; then tell me what you would like me to do for
them today. Pray very, very much. Don't stop asking.
I like generous hearts that come to forget themselves,
in a certain way, so as to help others in their needs.

"Talk to me like this, simply and informally, about the poor you want to console, the sick you see suffering, the wayward you want to return to the right path, the absent friends you would like to see at your side once again.

"For all of them, speak to me in tones of friendship and affection and fervor. Remind me that I promised to listen to all your heartfelt pleas; and wouldn't it be a heartfelt prayer when you intercede for those your heart especially loves?

"And for you, do you need any particular grace? If you want, make me a list of your needs, then come and read it to me in my presence. Tell me frankly that you feel proud, that you are too inclined to sensuality and entitlement; that you are perhaps selfish, inconstant, negligent....

"And then ask me to help you in your efforts, be they few or many, to get rid of these defects.

"Do not be ashamed, poor soul! There are so many just men and women, so many top-notch saints who had those same defects! But they prayed with humility... and little by little they were freed of them.

"Don't hesitate to ask me for spiritual and bodily goods: health, memory, success in your work, business, or studies; I can give you all of that and I do give it, and I want you to ask it of me as long as it is not against your sanctification, but fosters and helps it. Today, what do you need? What can I do for your good? If you knew how much I want to help you prosper! [...]

"And for me? Don't you feel the desire for me to be glorified? Wouldn't you like to do something good for your neighbors, your friends, those whom you love so much, and who perhaps live forgetful of me? And don't you perhaps have some joyful news to tell me about? Why don't you share it with me as with a good friend? Tell me about what has consoled you and made your heart smile since yesterday, since the last visit you made to me. [...] All of this is my work, and I have given it to you. [...] Tell me simply, as a child to its father: "Thank you, my Father, thank you!" Thanksgiving brings new benefits, since the giver of gifts likes to see that his gifts are appreciated.

"And don't you also have some promise to make to me? [...] You already know that I can read your heart's depths. [...] Talk to me, then, in all sincerity. Do you have a firm resolution not to expose yourself anymore to that occasion of sin? [...] Not to have any more dealings with that person who disturbs the peace of your soul? Will you become sweet, kind, and considerate to that person who faulted against you, and whom even today you see as an enemy?

"Now then, my child, go back to your usual occupations, to the workshop, the family, your studies...; but don't forget the fifteen minutes of pleasant conversation we have had here, just the two of us [...]. Love my Mother, who is also your Mother, the Blessed Virgin, and come back tomorrow with a more loving heart that is even more dedicated to serving me.

"In my heart you will find new love, new benefits, new consolations every day."

Adapted from
"Fifteen minutes with Jesus
in the Blessed Sacrament."

CPSIA information can be obtained
at www.ICGtesting.com
Printed in the USA
BVHW07s0429260618
519601BV00006B/8/P